Welcome to America's Historic Triangle

The story told in America's Historic Triangle has, like all good stories, a beginning, a middle, and an end. The seeds of the nation sown in the wilderness of Jamestown Island bore fruit in the Revolutionary city of Williamsburg, fruit harvested on the battlefields of Yorktown.

The story opened in 1607 when Jamestown became the first permanent English settlement in North America. Here Indian, English, and African peoples met and shaped a New World. Twelve years later, after enduring extraordinary hardships, the early colonists elected the first representative assembly in English America.

That government survived crisis upon crisis. It moved inland to Middle Plantation. The lawmakers rechristened that place Williamsburg, a new capital for a new century. Here young men—George Washington, George Wythe, Thomas Jefferson, George Mason, Patrick Henry, and Richard Henry Lee, among others—wrestled with the representatives of the British king for their rights. Ultimately, in May 1776, in the Capitol at the end of Duke of Gloucester Street, they determined no longer to be subjects of a monarch but instead to be citizens of an independent nation.

The Revolution that ensued brought years of suffering and war that, again, culminated right here in the Historic Triangle. In 1781, General Washington rode from Williamsburg to Yorktown, where his forces aided by French allies redeemed America's claim on independence.

From Jamestown, from Williamsburg, from Yorktown came a new nation. The story of America's Historic Triangle is a compelling one. But, like all great stories, its end was not truly the end. For America was more than a new nation—it was a new idea. Our American experiment in self-government, launched here in the Historic Triangle, continues today.

We hope you enjoy visiting the places where our nation was born . . . and we hope it inspires y

...........burg Foundation

JAMESTOWN
WILLIAMSBURG
YORKTOWN

The Official Guide to
America's
HISTORIC
TRIANGLE

SECOND EDITION

Colonial Williamsburg
The Colonial Williamsburg Foundation
Williamsburg, Virginia
www.history.org
in association with
John F. Blair, Publisher
Winston-Salem, North Carolina
www.blairpub.com

© 2010 by The Colonial Williamsburg Foundation
All rights reserved. First edition 2007
Second edition 2010

ISBN: 978-0-87935-246-2

Printed in Singapore

20 19 18 17 16 15 14 13 12 11 10   1 2 3 4 5 6 7 8

The Library of Congress has cataloged the first edition as follows:

Jamestown, Williamsburg, Yorktown : the official guide to America's historic
triangle.
     p. cm.
  Includes index.
  ISBN-13: 978-0-87935-230-1 (pbk. : alk. paper)
  ISBN-10: 0-87935-230-2 (pbk. : alk. paper) 1. Jamestown (Va.)—Guidebooks. 2.
Williamsburg (Va.)—Guidebooks. 3. Yorktown (Va.)—Guidebooks. 4. James-
town Region (Va.)—Guidebooks. 5. Williamsburg Region (Va.)—Guidebooks.
6. Yorktown Region (Va.)—Guidebooks. I. Colonial Williamsburg Foundation.
II. Title.

  F234.J3J36 2007
  973.2'1--dc22

                    2006036499

Designed by Helen M. Olds

Cover photography by David M. Doody and Barbara Lombardi
Frontispiece: Jamestown Settlement's re-created *Godspeed,* photo by Barbara
Lombardi

Colonial Williamsburg®, Colonial Williamsburg Historic Trades®, Christiana
Campbell's Tavern®, Chowning's Tavern®, King's Arms Tavern®, Shields Tavern®,
Williamsburg®, Williamsburg At Home®, Williamsburg Booksellers®,
Williamsburg Collection®, Williamsburg Inn®, Williamsburg Marketplace®, and
Revolutionary City® are trademarks of The Colonial Williamsburg Foundation, a
not-for-profit educational institution.

Published by The Colonial Williamsburg Foundation, PO Box 1776, Williamsburg, VA 23187-1776 in association with John F. Blair, Publisher, 1406 Plaza
Drive, Winston-Salem, NC 27103

www.history.org
www.blairpub.com

Sun – Aug 12th
  Check In
   Groceries

Mon ⎫
           Bush Gardens
Tues ⎪
           VA Beach
Wed ⎬
           Historic Downtown
Th ⎪
           Williamsburg Winery
Fri ⎭

           VA Aquarium
Sat – Pack   www.vmsm.com

Sun – Check out – 10 AM

Powhatan Creek Trail

Williamsburg Botanical
                    Garden
    in Freedom Park
    Butterfly Garden

Colonial Parkway

Contents

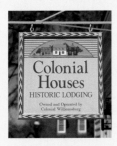

Practical Information

Planning Your Trip

THE HISTORIC TRIANGLE

Jamestown. Williamsburg. Yorktown. Three places, each of which can reasonably claim to be the place where America was born.

The first permanent English settlers arrived at Jamestown in 1607. This is where John Smith met Pocahontas, where the settlers traded and clashed with Indians led by chiefs such as Powhatan and Opechancanough, where the first representative legislative assembly in the New World met, where African slaves arrived.

At Williamsburg, the ideas of independence and revolution took form. Leaders such as George Washington, Thomas Jefferson, Patrick Henry, George Mason, and George Wythe all came to Williamsburg and there shaped the ideas about rights and responsibilities that transformed English into Americans, subjects into citizens.

The siege of Yorktown in 1781 was the last major battle of the American Revolution. Once George Washington's troops (aided by America's French allies) forced the surrender of the British, independence was inevitable.

In the Historic Triangle, Europeans, Indians, and Africans came together, and the eventual result was the United States of America. Had the Jamestown settlers returned to England, had the Williamsburg Revolutionaries been less resolute, had British general Lord Cornwallis and his troops escaped Yorktown, this could have been a very different nation.

What emerged from the Historic Triangle was a new kind of nation and a new kind of citizenship. By visiting Historic James-towne (see page 89), Jamestown Settlement (see page 109), Colonial Williamsburg's Historic Area (see page 139), Yorktown Battlefield (see page 185), and the Yorktown Victory Center (see page 195), you are joining this continuing experiment in democracy.

OTHER ATTRACTIONS

Not far from the Historic Triangle are numerous other historic sites, as well as beaches, theme parks, and championship golf courses. In Richmond, for

example, is St. John's Church (see page 220), where Patrick Henry proclaimed, "Give me liberty or give me death." Right outside Charlottesville is Monticello (see pages 225–226), Thomas Jefferson's mountaintop home. In Newport News is the Mariners' Museum (see pages 208–209), the largest maritime museum in North America. And, right in the Historic Triangle are Busch Gardens and Water Country USA (see pages 203–204), with dozens of thrilling rides.

FIND YOUR WAY . . . AND STAY AWHILE

The Historic Triangle is in Tidewater Virginia, just 150 miles southeast of Washington, D.C., and about an hour's drive from either Richmond or Norfolk. The Triangle is easily reached via Interstates 95 and 64, U.S. Route 17, and scenic Route 5. Newport News/Williamsburg, Norfolk, and Richmond International Airports are all nearby and have car rental and limousine services. Amtrak and Greyhound arrive and depart from the Williamsburg Transportation Center, just blocks from Colonial Williamsburg's Historic Area. Look for the red, white, and blue directional signs throughout the Historic Triangle area. All three points on the Historic Triangle are connected by the Colonial Parkway, a scenic drive along the James and York Rivers.

The best way to start your trip to the Historic Triangle is with a visit to Colonial Williamsburg's Visitor Center, located at a midpoint on the Colonial Parkway. The Visitor Center serves as a regional hub for tourists. There are multimedia displays about the area's historic sites and other attractions; ticketing, dining, and lodging help; and information about special events and recreation options. The Visitor Center also offers free parking.

Colonial Williamsburg's official hotels and conference facilities are located right next to the Historic Area and its museums, taverns, and golf courses.

When It All Happened

May 14, 1607: BEGINNINGS
The English come ashore and begin building Jamestown.

December 1607: RESCUE
John Smith meets Powhatan and is saved by Pocahontas.

Winter 1609–1610: DEATH
Only sixty settlers survive the Starving Time, down from about five hundred.

April 5, 1614: LOVE
Pocahontas marries John Rolfe, leading to peace between the English and Indians.

July 30–August 4, 1619: DEMOCRACY
The first representative assembly in the New World meets at Jamestown.

August 1619: SLAVERY
The first Africans arrive in Jamestown.

March 22, 1622: WAR
Opechancanough leads an Indian attack that kills about one-third of the English settlers.

September 19, 1676: REBELLION
Nathaniel Bacon's forces burn Jamestown.

1699: CAPITAL
The capital is moved from Jamestown to Williamsburg.

May 30, 1765: THUNDER
Patrick Henry delivers his "Caesar had his Brutus" speech in opposition to the Stamp Act.

June 1, 1774: PRAYER
Virginians observe a day of "Fasting, Humiliation, and Prayer" after the British close the port of Boston.

August 1–6, 1774: CONGRESS
Virginians choose delegates, including Peyton Randolph, George Washington, and Patrick Henry, to send to the first congress of all the colonies, which meets in September.

November 7, 1774: TEA
Almost a year after the Boston Tea Party, Virginians throw chests of tea into the York River.

March 17, 1775: LIBERTY
Patrick Henry delivers his "give me liberty or give me death" speech at a meeting of the legislature in Richmond.

April 21, 1775: GUNS
Days after the battles of Lexington and Concord, British marines seize the colonists' arms and ammunition in Williamsburg.

June 8, 1775: FLIGHT
     The last British governor, Lord Dunmore, leaves
     Williamsburg.

May 15, 1776: REVOLUTION
     Virginians instruct delegates in Congress to introduce a
     motion for independence.

June 12, 1776: RIGHTS
     Virginians enact America's first bill of rights, George Mason's
     Declaration of Rights.

June 29, 1776: CONSTITUTION
     Virginia, no longer a British colony, adopts a constitution,
     and Patrick Henry is elected governor.

July 25, 1776: INDEPENDENCE
     Days after it's signed in Philadelphia, the Declaration of
     Independence is read in Williamsburg.

April 18, 1781: TRAITOR
     Benedict Arnold, now a British general, burns the Chicka-
     hominy shipyard outside Williamsburg.

May 10, 1781: INVASION
     British forces under General Cornwallis enter Virginia.

June 4, 1781: ESCAPE
     Thomas Jefferson, who has succeeded Henry as governor,
     avoids capture by hiding in the woods near Monticello.

August 1, 1781: OCCUPATION
     Cornwallis's forces set up camp in Yorktown, planning to use
     it as a base for further attacks in Virginia.

September 5, 1781: BATTLE
     A French fleet forces a British fleet to return to New York,
     leaving Cornwallis trapped in Yorktown.

September 14, 1781: ARRIVAL
     Washington reaches Williamsburg.

September 28, 1781: MARCH
     The American and French armies leave from Williamsburg
     for Yorktown.

September 30, 1781: SIEGE
     The British surrender their outermost earthworks.

October 14, 1781: REDOUBTS
     American and French forces capture Redoubts No. 9 and
     No. 10, key British defensive positions.

October 16, 1781: STORM
     Cornwallis's forces attempt to escape across the York River,
     but a sudden storm forces them back to Yorktown.

October 19, 1781: VICTORY
     Cornwallis officially surrenders, ending the last major battle
     of the Revolution.

September 3, 1783: PEACE
     The Treaty of Paris formally ends the Revolution and estab-
     lishes American independence.

Where It All Began

WHAT HAPPENED
AT JAMESTOWN

*W*hat was America like before Europeans arrived? What was it like before Leif Eriksson saw Newfoundland more than a thousand years ago, before Christopher Columbus thought he found a back door to India, before John and Sebastian Cabot explored North America, before Hernando Cortés conquered the Aztecs in Mexico or Francisco Pizarro the Incas in Peru? We have fresh evidence of people, having arrived from the west, living here in the tidewater area of what is now called Virginia at least fifteen or sixteen thousand years ago. These Indian people, too, were once immigrants. We Americans are all immigrants, every one of us, and the ones who got here first forgot to close the door.

The Englishmen who arrived in Virginia in 1607 came ashore on a land ruled by Wahunsonacock, also known as Powhatan. He had taken on the name Powhatan, the village in which he was born, when he became ruler. The peoples he ruled, who represented over thirty different tribes, were also known collectively as the Powhatans. Powhatan inherited his chiefdom sometime after 1570 and then moved to expand and consolidate his power. By the time the English arrived, Powhatan ruled from south of the James River to as far north as the Potomac, from the Chesapeake Bay to as far west as present-day Richmond. The Indians called this land Tsenacommacah. There were about fifteen thousand people here, living in hundreds of towns, many along the area's waterways, the highways of the time.

Powhatan was powerful but not all-powerful. While the peoples of Tsenacommacah generally supported him militarily, they had their own policies and were loyal to their own leaders, among them Powhatan's brother Opechancanough, chief of the Pamunkeys. (Remember Opechancanough; he'll be back.) The Pamunkeys made up the core of Powhatan's forces with a few hundred warriors. Powhatan, like other chiefs, also had to take into account the advice of his counselors and priests, especially before going to war. Had Powhatan launched a concerted attack on the three ships that anchored just off Jamestown Island on May 13, 1607, Jamestown might never have been.

The Peoples of Tsenacommacah

"Tsenacommacah" may have meant "densely inhabited land," and, while it was certainly not densely inhabited by modern standards, there were about fifteen thousand people living here before the English arrived. The Powhatans belonged to more than thirty tribes, with villages up and down the James, York, Mattaponi, Pamunkey, Rappahannock, and Potomac Rivers, as well as their tributaries.

Each tribe had its own werowance (chief), the most powerful of whom was Wahunsonacock, better known as Powhatan. Other Indians paid tribute to Powhatan, but, by 1607, he had only recently consolidated his power. Many of the peoples retained their own customs, dialects, and governments, and Powhatan's lack of complete control over them may have been one reason he didn't launch a concerted attack on the English. Nor were the English the only external threat to Powhatan's power; the Monacans were, until 1607, his only source for copper, and he may have traded with the English in part to lessen his dependence on that rival chiefdom.

The peoples of Tsenacommacah had in common their ability to live off the land, primarily by farming but also by hunting, fishing, and gathering. In the spring, they ate fish, oysters, wild berries, and small animals; in summer, there were fish, small game, fruits and berries, green corn, and squash; in the early fall, corn, beans, squash, game, and waterfowl; and, in late fall, dried corn, beans, nuts, wild turkeys, and waterfowl. Food was sparser in winter, but there were tubers and nuts.

Hunting and fishing were men's work. The Powhatans hunted with bows and arrows and clubs. They fished in dugout canoes or waded in shallow water, using spears or fishhooks made from bone and tied to fishing lines. They also used nets woven of cord made from bark, grass, or sinew. Future leaders experienced the huskanaw ritual, nine months of living in isolation in the forest.

Farming was women's work. To clear their fields, the Powhatans would first slash the bark of trees to kill them and then burn acres at a time. The English didn't think much of women farmers, or of the slash-and-burn techniques that left stumps among the fields. But, these Indian farmers had more control over their lives than most English-women, and their fields produced plenty of fresh vegetables from July through October.

The Powhatans didn't wear much clothing, even in the winter. They wore deer hides, often decorated with fringe, beads, bones, teeth, and paint. Powhatan homes, called "yehakins," varied in size and shape and covering, with some small and round and others oblong. The frames were created from young saplings and then covered with bark or reed mats that could be rolled up in warm weather.

Powhatans worshipped a variety of gods. The greatest was Ahone, the giver of good things, who created the world and the other gods.

The language they spoke is extinct, though we know Englishmen like John Smith and William Strachey recorded a few words, such as "moccasin." The people themselves continue to this day, despite years of war followed by centuries of racism. The Commonwealth of Virginia today recognizes eight Powhatan tribes: Monacan, Chickahominy, Eastern Chickahominy, Mattaponi, Nansemond, Pamunkey, United Rappahannock, and Upper Mattaponi. Some Pamunkey and Mattaponi people still live on reservations west of the town of West Point.

Town of Secota from Theodore de Bry, *Grands Voyages,* Frankfurt, Germany, 1590. Letters for key in original.

1991 replica of the *Susan Constant*.

Those aboard the *Susan Constant,* the *Godspeed,* and the *Discovery* had looked at five possible settlement sites along the James since May 4, but they preferred these Indian hunting grounds. It was far enough from the coast to allay worries about a surprise Spanish attack, and the water that surrounded the island (except for a narrow land bridge) made it easier to defend should the Spanish arrive. A channel was deep enough to let the English dock near the land (and keep their shipboard cannons handy). On May 14, about 104 men and boys came ashore. In some accounts, you will read of these intrepid men and boys wading ashore. Colorful, to be sure, but highly unlikely. Small boats that took them from ship to shore are a lot more likely. And drier.

The settlers had boarded the *Susan Constant,* the *Discovery*, and the *Godspeed* at Blackwall, downriver from London, in late 1606. They spent six weeks anchored just off the English coast, tossed about by cold, stormy weather. They finally set sail when decent weather arrived in February 1607. They used the southern route through the Canary Islands and then west to the Caribbean and north to Virginia, arriving in the Chesapeake Bay on April 26, 1607.

The voyage was not a flight to freedom and liberty but a commercial venture, a way to make money. Every one of the settlers hoped for a substantial profit.

So did the Virginia Company of London, which sponsored the voyage. Spain was already in the Americas, mostly South and Central America, and finding gold and silver. Spain considered the Atlantic her very own pond and the

Aerial view of Jamestown Island.

Americas her very own playground. England wanted to share in the riches of the New World. One way to get at those riches was through privateering—a government-sanctioned sort of pirating—but, when peace with Spain broke out in 1604, that put a stop to that. The English had made a couple of earlier attempts at settling North America, but they had failed. Some of the settlers went home; some of them died; some of them disappeared. London's leaders were willing to try again, especially if it might make money. In 1606, the Virginia Company of London's organizers won King James I's permission to found a settlement.

Seal of the Virginia Company of London.

Why were these English people, not the leaders and investors, willing to go across the ocean to a new land? For the same reason—to make money. The Virginia Company assured settlers that America was a wonderful place with endless opportunity. In England, there were inflation, low wages, unemployment, and a growing population on a finite amount of land. As archaeologist Ivor Noël Hume observed, "Few, if any [of the settlers] believed that the future promised worse than the past." On December 20, 1606, these men and boys set out for that future.

It was not a fun voyage. The settlers had been aboard in rough weather, often seasick, before they sailed. The ships were jammed and smelly, and the sanitary and medical facilities minimal at best. There was no such thing as a bath, so the settlers bathed in the rivers of the Canaries and the West Indies when the ships stopped there. The only man who died on the journey succumbed to heatstroke during one of the stops. At sea, the toilet was a couple of planks off the bow of the ship. But, if you wanted to get to America, a ship was the only way, no matter how time-consuming, uncomfortable, and crowded.

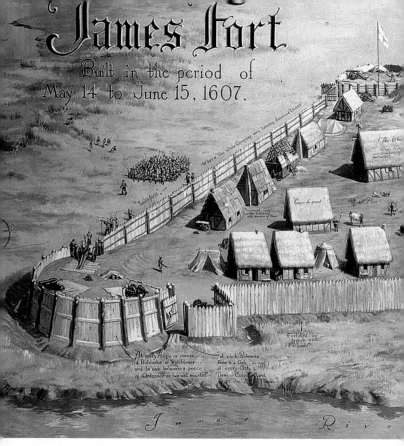

James Fort

Built in the period of
May 14 to June 15, 1607.

James Fort by Sidney King, ca. 1957.

The settlers might have been more apprehensive if they had known that their leaders, whose names the company had sealed in a box to be opened on arrival, were arguing among themselves. The two who fought the most were Edward Maria Wingfield and John Smith. Smith was a short, tough mercenary who'd been enslaved briefly in Turkey, a man who wrote extensively (but not always consistently) about his experience and perhaps was too sure that he knew how to do it, whatever "it" was. Wingfield was a wellborn blowhard, absolutely certain of his own worth and place ahead of others and surely ahead of a commoner like Smith. He was wealthy, a charter investor in the Virginia Company, and he had two servants with him. Wingfield seemed unable to take advice or counsel from anyone, and Smith seemed unable not to give it. If ever two men were destined to not get along, they were Wingfield and Smith.

Their dislike of each other got out of hand after the ships took on fresh water in the Canaries, and the imperious Wingfield had the plain-born Smith locked up. The charge was that he intended "to usurpe the government, murder the Councell, and make himselfe king."

During the first few years this was the town of Jamestown. According to an early account the fort was cast almost into the forme of a Triangle and so Pallizadoed.

The Virginia Company had written instructions to be opened after the ships' arrival in Virginia. When they opened the box, the settlers learned that a seven-man council would administer Jamestown. The president was Edward Maria Wingfield. The other council members were Christopher Newport, commander of the *Susan Constant;* Bartholomew Gosnold, a Virginia Company originator and commander of the *Godspeed;* John Ratcliffe, commander of the *Discovery;* a couple of well-connected, wealthy settlers named George Kendall and John Martin; and John Smith, the man under arrest.

Within a year, Wingfield went home in disgrace. Smith took over and saved the colony again and again, and, even though his part seemed larger each time he told of it, he probably did save it.

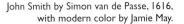

John Smith by Simon van de Passe, 1616, with modern color by Jamie May.

19

Where Are the Pilgrims?

The short answer is: not here.

More intriguing is why so many Americans think of the Pilgrims, who landed at Plymouth, Massachusetts, in 1620—fully thirteen years after John Smith and company founded Jamestown—as English America's first colonists. If you think Plymouth Rock is somehow a sturdier story about the nation's origins than the much-disputed tales of Pocahontas and John Smith, think again: it wasn't until 1741, more than a hundred years after the Pilgrims landed, that ninety-five-year-old Elder Faunce mentioned the rock on which his ancestors allegedly came ashore.

One reason Plymouth captured the popular imagination was the Mayflower Compact. This document, signed by forty-one passengers aboard the ship about to dock at Plymouth, bound them to abide by any laws they'd later pass. Later generations would tout it as a forerunner to the Declaration of Independence or the Constitution, conveniently forgetting that it also bound them to follow the dictates of King James. Jamestown had no equivalent.

Plymouth Rock also made a fine metaphor. In 1774, on the eve of the Revolution, some citizens of Plymouth decided the rock would be better preserved on higher ground. As a team of oxen tugged, the rock split in half. "The separation of the rock," James Thacher's 1835 history explained, "was construed to be ominous of a division of the British Empire." To protect the portion they'd removed from the harbor, the citizens of Plymouth surrounded it with an iron fence. And Plymouth's tourist trade benefited from the town's continued prosperity. Jamestown, in contrast, became largely farmland after Williamsburg became the capital. Only a church tower remained to remind visitors that this was once a bustling town.

It was during the years leading up to the Civil War that the competition between Jamestown and Plymouth really heated up. Northerners stressed the moral rectitude of the industrious Pilgrims and made fun of John Smith's dependence on a half-naked Indian girl. Southerners countered with a family-oriented emphasis on the marriage between John Rolfe and Pocahontas. This was an uplifting tale of interracial harmony, and it might have had a greater impact had the South not also been the home of slavery.

Above all, what Plymouth had going for it was its very own holiday. True, Virginians argued that the first Thanksgiving actually took place at Berkeley Plantation, just a few miles up the James River from Jamestown. It was there, in 1619, that thirty-eight settlers came ashore and proclaimed that "the day of our ships arrivall at the place assigned for plantacon in the land of Virginia shall by yearly and perputualy keept holy as a day of thanksgiving to Almighty god." And, true, there's no evidence that the Pilgrims, after sharing their 1621 harvest with the Wampanoags, held any sort of similar annual event or that the original feast had any sort of connection to the national holiday. But, as a national holiday, Thanksgiving was most definitely more of a Northern celebration: Abraham Lincoln declared the first national day of thanksgiving in 1863 after a series of Union victories.

So, the historical reality aside, a great many people will continue to think of Plymouth as the site of the first permanent English settlement in America. Rather than displacing the Pilgrims, we may have to settle for deflating them, as Mark Twain did in 1881. "The Pilgrims were a simple and ignorant race," Twain told the New England Society of Philadelphia. "They never had seen any good rocks before, or at least any that were not watched, and so they were excusable for hopping ashore in frantic delight and clapping an iron fence around this one."

The colony needed lots of saving. Remember the six weeks on board before they sailed? For those six weeks, they ate the food that had been intended for when they arrived, so they were short of supplies from the first day. And the Indians whose lands they invaded were not always welcoming. Sometimes they would trade food for the tools and beads the settlers had; other times they would not. Early on, about two hundred warriors attacked the settlers and were driven off by cannons. That was the only report of an Indian attack in force against the settlers in the early years, although both sides made sporadic small raids.

Christopher Newport took the *Susan Constant* and the *Godspeed* back to London in late June but left the *Discovery* to be used for exploration around the Chesapeake Bay. The men and boys—no women yet—set out to make money and survive. Most of them did

King Powhatan comands C: Smith to be slame, his daughter Pokahontas beggs his life his thankfullnes and how he subiected 39 of their kings. reade history.

printed by Iames Reeve

Rescue of John Smith by Pocahontas from Smith's *Generall Historie,* London, 1624.

neither, including Bartholomew Gosnold, commander of the *Godspeed,* who stayed behind to help lead the settlers but died in August. When the next group of settlers arrived from England in January 1608, only 38 of the original 104 were alive.

Among the instructions from the Virginia Company was to select a site that was "the Strongest most Fertile and wholesome place." The settlers did not do that. Indeed, they didn't even come close. The island was, essentially, a mosquito-infested marsh with a tainted water supply, so fevers and dysentery were constant. The record of deaths never misses a week, and rarely misses more than a couple of days. One of the dead might have been John Smith, except for Pocahontas. At least, that's the story that has been told to schoolchildren for years, a story that even Chief Justice John Marshall repeated in 1804.

In December 1607, Smith led a trading party up the Chickahominy River. He was captured by Powhatan's brother Opechancanough. Some days later, Smith wound up in front of Powhatan, who had to decide what to do with this interloper. Smith and Powhatan lied to each other for a while, and Powhatan fed Smith rather well.

Here's how Smith, in his 1624 *Generall Historie of Virginia, New-England, and the Summer Isles* (and referring to himself in the third person), described what happened next:

> A long consultation was held, but the conclusion was, two great stones were brought before Powhatan: then as many as could layd hands on him, dragged him to them, and thereon laid his head, and being ready with their clubs, to beate out his braines, Pocahontas the Kings dearest daughter, when no intreaty could prevaile, got his head in her armes, and laid her owne upon his to save him from death: whereat the Emperour was contented he should live to make him hatchets, and her bells.

By this account, Pocahontas, then a girl, probably not much more than ten years old, made sure the only way Powhatan could kill Smith was by killing his own daughter first. He couldn't do that, so Smith was spared. He was released two days later in exchange for the promise of "two great gunnes, and a gryndstone." Powhatan declared that Smith was now his "sonne."

Why did Pocahontas save Smith's life? Smith thought it was compassion for a man in distress. Others have credited love or infatuation. Still others have said Smith made up the whole story, or at least greatly exaggerated. Now comes a modern interpretation: Based, at least in part, on Powhatan's declaration that Smith was now equal to a son, the threatened head bashing was not really a death threat but some sort of adoption ceremony. Pocahontas rushed forward to protect Smith as part of a carefully scripted maneuver. Might be.

There is no disagreement about the next milestone in the story of Jamestown: the arrival of the first women. That was September 1608. Thomas Forrest, a gentleman, arrived with his wife to settle at Jamestown. With them was Mrs. Forrest's maid, Anne Buras. Mrs. Forrest disappears from the written record, but the unmarried maid shows up. One can only guess at her popularity, the only single English woman there. By the end of the year, Anne Buras married John Laydon, a carpenter, and the couple eventually had four daughters, the first of whom was named—what else?—Virginia. Mrs. Laydon was still alive in 1625, which was no mean accomplishment given how many others were by then dead.

The year women arrived was also the year Smith, in a mere barge and with only a dozen or so men, undertook a series of explorations of the Chesapeake Bay. By his own account, he conquered thirty-five Indian kings. This is probably an exaggeration; most of the Indians he encountered gave him food and information as part of a trade, not a tribute. What the voyages did make clear was that neither the Chesapeake nor its rivers would take them to the Pacific Ocean and that, unlike their Spanish counterparts, these Englishmen's way would not be eased by the discovery of gold.

Smith almost died in 1609 when his gunpowder bag, worn around his waist, caught fire. Smith had enemies from the beginning, but we don't know whether this was by accident or design. He put out the fire by jumping into the river. The burning gunpowder left about nine square inches of his thigh deeply wounded, and there was no doctor at Jamestown. Smith sailed back to London, never to return to the Virginia Colony. He would write about Virginia and support Virginia, but he would never go back.

At the beginning of October 1609, with Smith gone, there were three months of rations, not nearly enough to make it through the winter. The extent of the settlers' hunger and their desperation during the winter of 1609–1610 show in the fact that at least some of them turned to cannibalism. Their storehouse was empty, and, when settlers left the fort to find food, they found waiting warriors instead. This winter came to be known as the Starving Time.

Wrote George Percy, the colony's governor at the time: "Now all of us att James Towne beginneinge to feele that sharpe pricke of hunger wch noe man trewly descrybe butt he wch hath Tasted the bitternesse thereof A worlde of miseries ensewed." In the fall of 1609, the population of Jamestown was about five hundred; when supply ships arrived in May 1610, it was down to sixty.

What went wrong? You might want to consider the different theories. It could change how you think of the settlers. Older histories, following the lead of John Smith, have generally blamed the gentlemen in the ranks of the settlers—between a third and a half—who would not work with their hands and, even if they would, did not know how to do anything.

Artifacts found at Jamestown: German stoneware, 1607–1609 James I halfpenny (page 26), and thimble found at James Fort (page 27).

Smith ordered, "He that will not worke shall not eate." (One wonders if the Anglican Smith got that from Second Thessalonians 3:10: "If any would not work, neither should he eat.")

Newer research points to various environmental factors. The island in the James River may have offered some protection from Spanish and Indian attacks, and it was a very pretty place. Come summer, though, Jamestown became a swamp, surrounded by stagnant and brackish water. This was the water the colonists drank, and it made them sick. They didn't have any choice since Indians had sealed off the island.

One of the most persuasive explanations for the colonists' plight came after scientists measured tree rings in southeastern Virginia. The width of each ring indicates how much a tree grew that year, so the rings are a good indication of the annual rainfall. Data taken from bald cypress trees indicate that Jamestown was settled during one of the most severe droughts of the past eight hundred years. The droughts affected the Indians as well, limiting how much corn the tribes had to trade.

As archaeologist Dennis Blanton put it, "If it weren't for bad luck, these English wouldn't have had any luck at all."

John Rolfe, who was eventually responsible for the financial success of the Virginia Colony, could have been present for the Starving Time, but he was not. Rolfe and his first wife were passengers on the *Sea Venture,* part of a supply fleet bound for Virginia. The *Sea Venture* wrecked on Bermuda during a nasty storm. Bermuda, uninhabited then, was a lovely place, filled with hogs, turtles, fruits, berries, and all the fish you could take. The ship also had on board Sir George Somers, the admiral, and Sir Thomas Gates, Virginia's lieutenant governor. Those two had the passengers salvage the *Sea Venture,* stuck on a reef less than a mile out, and cut new timber and build two new ships, the *Deliverance,* forty feet, and the *Patience,* twenty-nine feet. It took nine months, but the job got done. During those months, Mrs. Rolfe had a baby girl, named Bermuda. Mother and child both died on the island.

The Tempest

A fleet of nine ships set sail from England in June 1609, its mission to bring supplies and settlers to the two-year-old colony at Jamestown. In command was George Somers, a successful privateer turned country gentleman and an officer and investor in the Virginia Company. Somers was on board the *Sea Venture,* as was Thomas Gates, who had been appointed lieutenant governor of the colony.

About seven days' sail from Virginia, the *Sea Venture* encountered a hurricane. William Strachey, a passenger on the *Sea Venture* and an experienced traveler, said that all the other storms he'd "suffered gathered together might not hold comparison with this: there was not a moment in which the sudden splitting or instant over-setting of the ship was not expected."

After three hellish days of plugging holes and bailing water, Somers managed to wedge the ship into a reef off the coast of Bermuda. The crew and passengers ferried to land. Amazingly, all 150 on board made it safely.

Bermuda was deserted but no desert. To their surprise and delight, the castaways discovered the island was, as *Sea Venture* passenger Silvester Jourdain put it, "the richest, healthfullest, and [most] pleasing land ... as ever man set foot upon." There was plenty of food for the marooned, including fish, large tortoises, and hogs, which had survived an earlier shipwreck.

Life on the island was full and eventful: it included one murder, one execution, three mutinies, one marriage, and two births. The baby girl, Bermuda Rolfe, who, along with her mother, died on the island, was the daughter of John Rolfe, who would later marry Pocahontas. What sparked the mutinies was that some of the castaways had no desire to leave Bermuda since they realized life in Jamestown might not be nearly as pleasant. Some questioned whether Somers and Gates had any authority over them since Somers was in charge of a ship that no longer existed and Gates was in charge of a colony six hundred miles away.

Still, Somers insisted that they fulfill their original mission, and he and Gates supervised the construction of two ships made from Bermudan cedar and beams and planks salvaged from the *Sea Venture* and other wrecks. In May 1610, the colonists again set sail, this time aboard the newly christened *Deliverance* and *Patience*. They arrived in Jamestown a few weeks later.

The voyage of the *Sea Venture* had literary as well as historic significance. Two accounts by castaways, one by Strachey and the other by Jourdain, were quickly circulated and became the talk of London. Some scholars believe the story inspired William Shakespeare to write *The Tempest*. Prospero's island was set in the Caribbean, not the Atlantic, but colonization was clearly one of the play's themes, and there were plenty of indications—Ariel's mention of "the still-vex'd Bermoothes," for example—that Shakespeare knew about Somers's journey. *The Tempest* was first performed in 1611, just a few months after Somers died.

When the former Bermuda castaways finally made it to Jamestown, it was clear they did not carry enough food to save the colony. Jamestown's survivors clambered aboard for the return trip to England, abandoning Jamestown. The town appeared destined to join Roanoke Island to the south as another "lost colony." As the ships sailed down the James River toward the Chesapeake Bay, they ran into another fleet, this one commanded by the new governor of Virginia, Thomas West, Lord De La Warr. West brought with him food and supplies, and he ordered the settlers back to Jamestown. The first permanent English-speaking settlement in the New World survived.

It was Rolfe who, by 1613 or so, developed a Virginia tobacco that was much milder than the usually harsh American plant. Even before then, tobacco was gaining popularity in Europe, where it was used to treat colds, asthma, and a variety of other ailments. Virginia tobacco caught on and became the colony's cash crop of choice, replacing the futile hunt for gold and ensuring the financial success of the colony. That alone should have made Rolfe famous. He is best remembered, however, not for tobacco, but for Pocahontas. He married her.

This was hardly a standard courtship. In the spring of 1613, Pocahontas was visiting friends. Capt. Samuel Argall, on a trading mission, heard Pocahontas was in the area. He approached an Indian, Iopassus, and told him of his plan to take her hostage in return for English prisoners held by Powhatan. Through a combination of threats and bribes, Argall convinced Iopassus to cooperate. Iopassus and his wife in turn convinced Pocahontas to board Argall's ship for a supper. The next morning, Iopassus and his wife left, but Pocahontas was forced to stay.

Powhatan freed some prisoners, but the English held onto Pocahontas. Pocahontas went to live with the English, where Rolfe met her. He wrote a letter to Gov. Thomas Dale, who took over as leader of the colony in 1611, asking to be allowed to marry this heathen woman to help convert her to Christianity.

Tobacco pipe bowls.

She would be given the name Rebecca, the beautiful foreign girl who was a sign of God's blessing of Abraham. The governor agreed. Pocahontas and Rolfe were not the first people in history whose marriage brought peace. They may, however, have been among the few who actually liked each other. They were married in April 1614. Powhatan did not attend, but he sent one of Pocahontas's uncles and two of his sons. Two peaceful years later, after Dale decided it might be a good way to promote the colony, Rolfe, Rebecca, and their infant son, Thomas, sailed to England on the *Treasurer*. The captain was Samuel Argall, the man who had kidnapped Pocahontas.

The Marriage of Pocahontas by John C. McRae, after Henry Brueckner, 1800s (above).

Pocahontas by C. Gregory Stapko after unknown artist, ca. 1958 (right).

The kidnapping ended well; the trip did not. As the Rolfe family was getting ready to return to Virginia on the *George,* Rebecca got sick. On March 21, 1617, she died at Gravesend, England, where she was buried at the church of St. George. Thomas was ill and was left with a friend in England. His father never saw him again although Thomas later returned to Virginia and became a respected and prosperous planter. John Rolfe, back in Virginia, married for a third time and was appointed secretary of the governing council.

Thirteen months after Pocahontas died in England, Powhatan died in the woods of Virginia of natural causes. It is possible to argue that, while he ruled, he made only one major mistake: he did not drive the English out while he could.

The next year, 1619, was a watershed year for Jamestown for three reasons, any one of which would have been historic. For all three to happen in one year is incredible. First, at the instruction of the Virginia Company in London, the new governor, Sir George Yeardley, began to distribute property—one hundred or fifty acres, depending on how long you'd been there—to the settlers "to be held by them their heirs and Assigns for ever." The free property was intended to give the new landowners reason to build houses and clear land and grow crops.

The next event was just as big, maybe bigger. The first elected representative government in the New World, the General Assembly, met at the Jamestown church on July 30, 1619. The Virginia Company wanted "a forme of government ther as may bee to the greatest benifitt and comfort of the people." The session ended quickly on August 4 because of the extreme heat, which may have had something to do with the death of one assemblyman. There were twenty men seated in the General Assembly when it started. We're not sure how they were elected, but we assume that women and male indentured servants did not have the vote, as they did not in England.

Did blacks have the vote? There were not any. Their arrival was the third major event of 1619.

At the end of August, the Dutch man-of-war *White Lion* arrived in Jamestown and traded, according to a letter written by John Rolfe, "20. and odd Negroes" for food. The 160-ton ship had partnered with the *Treasurer,* which it had met in the West Indies. (This was the same *Treasurer* that had carried John, Rebecca, and Thomas Rolfe to London.) The two had jumped a Portuguese ship in the Gulf of Mexico and taken some of the ship's cargo of slaves and then traded them in Virginia. It's not clear whether these Africans were sold as slaves or indentured servants. Even if they were indentured servants, however, these Africans certainly didn't enter into service of their own free will.

The arrival of the Africans was not necessarily the first meeting of white Europeans, American Indians, and Africans, but it was certainly the first prolonged meeting, the first time the three cultures were forced to live with each other. From that, the American people grew. It was not always easy or pleasant, and it happened over almost four hundred years. It's still going on.

The Powhatans, now led by Opechancanough, made two more concerted attempts to get rid of the English settlers, but they had waited too long. Too many settlers had arrived, building settlements on both sides of the James up and down the river from Jamestown. The first uprising was in 1622, and at least 347 settlers were killed by apparently friendly natives who used the settlers' own weapons to kill them. Jamestown, having been warned of the attack, fared better than the other settlements. The number of settlers killed was about a third, possibly more. Lest you believe the treachery was all on one side, at a peace treaty signing in May 1623, the colonists served the Indians poisoned wine, killing about two hundred of them. Fifty or so more were shot. A peace treaty wasn't signed until 1632.

"20. and odd Negroes"

It is one of the great paradoxes of our history that American freedom and American slavery both took root in Virginia. Indeed, it was just a few weeks after the establishment of the General Assembly in 1619 that the first Africans arrived. John Rolfe, in a letter he wrote a year later, described the arrival of the *White Lion,* a ship whose cargo was "not any thing but 20. and odd Negroes, wch the Governor and Cape Marchant bought [in exchange] for victualles."

These Africans were originally from the kingdom of Ndonga in Angola. Between 1618 and 1620, thousands of Ndongans were captured by Portuguese and sent to America as slaves. These particular Africans had been aboard a Portuguese ship bound for Mexico when the *White Lion* seized them.

What then happened to them has been the subject of much debate among historians. Though some undoubtedly ended up as slaves, others may have become indentured servants, working alongside whites of the same status. And, some, by one means or another, won their freedom. That was true for "Antonio a Negro," who arrived in 1621 and was sold to the Bennett family, owners of a tobacco plantation on the south side of the James River. He later changed his name to Anthony Johnson and moved to the Eastern Shore of Virginia. By 1651, Johnson owned more than 250 acres there and also a slave of his own.

There's other evidence that race relations in Virginia's early days were more flexible than later. Black and white servants often toiled side by side in the tobacco fields, and some married each other. Some black slaves earned money, sometimes saving enough to buy their freedom and occasionally suing for their freedom in Virginia courts. No precise numbers are available, but historians estimate that, in some Virginia counties in the middle of the seventeenth century, a third of blacks were free.

Still, from the start, there were signs of blatant racism. Early censuses compiled by the Virginia Company list first and last names of almost all whites, including servants. Of the twenty-three blacks in the 1624 census, ten are listed only by their first names. The remaining thirteen were given neither first nor last names, merely a dash followed by something like "one negar" or "A Negors Woman."

Even if some blacks held the same legal status as white indentured servants, the absence of any data on them in the census would seem to indicate their terms of service were indefinite. Besides, there was a huge difference between signing a contract, as did the whites, and being sold, as were the blacks. By the second half of the seventeenth century, prejudice had hardened into laws and customs that allowed blacks—free and enslaved—much less flexibility.

The Johnsons saw their freedoms shrinking. During the 1660s, they abandoned their land in Virginia and resettled in Maryland, Delaware, and New Jersey. Anthony Johnson's son and grandson settled in southern Delaware, where his grandson named the family estate "Angola."

Cast bronze plaque from Benin, Africa, ca. 1600 (above).

Ceramic memorial bust from West Africa, 1600–1800s (opposite).

Another casualty of the 1622 Indian uprising was the Virginia Company. King James revoked its charter in 1624 and made Virginia a royal colony, which it would be until the American Revolution, 151 years in the future.

Jamestown Massacre from Theodore de Bry, *Grands Voyages,* Frankfurt, Germany, 1626–1627.

The second uprising, also led by Opechancanough, was in the spring of 1644. It killed roughly five hundred settlers, but there were many more settlers by this time, so the attack did less harm than the one in 1622. There were the usual back-and-forth raids, and, in one of them, in 1646, Opechancanough was taken captive. He was almost certainly more than one hundred years old, unable to walk, carried around by his servants. He was taken to prison in Jamestown, where, as he lay helpless on his litter, one of his English guards shot him in the back. That was the end of the war and also the end of the Indians as a political force. As the General Assembly wrote, "They are no longer a nation, and we now suffer only from robbery by a few starved outlaws." From 1607 to 1646, Virginia's Indians lost their land, their leaders, their way of life, their independent future.

Meanwhile, the English arrived by the thousands. By 1650, the white population was eleven thousand, and settlers had taken up lands from the James to the Rappahannock River. At midcentury, there were still only a couple hundred Africans; poor white men and women labored in the tobacco fields.

The next chapter in the Jamestown story is Bacon's Rebellion. Some people have said the rebellion was the first step toward democracy, but that probably is an exaggeration. It was a hint or an omen, maybe, not a first step.

It was the summer of 1675, and some Indians raided some Virginia settlements. Virginia and Maryland militia volunteers went after them. There were excesses and killings on both sides. Virginia's royal governor, Sir William Berkeley, refused to send additional forces into the field, and people were angry because they believed Berkeley's refusal was to protect his own, private trading agreement with Indians for beaver fur. Nathaniel Bacon Jr., a cousin of Sir William's wife, took command of the rebel forces. Sir William talked tough but ran to the Eastern Shore across the Chesapeake Bay when Bacon's forces approached. In 1676 at Jamestown, Bacon set fire to town, church, and statehouse. Bacon took over the royal governor's estate and planned reforms, but he died suddenly of some sort of fever. The governor was restored to power and hanged two dozen men who had taken part in the revolt. In May 1677, Berkeley returned to London.

The statehouse was rebuilt in 1685 and burned again in 1698. People wanted "a healthier and more convenient Place, and freer from the Annoyance of *Muskettoes*," so, in 1699, the capital was moved from Jamestown to Middle Plantation, soon to be called Williamsburg.

It was Jamestown, however, that, as historian James Horn wrote, "became the first transatlantic site of an empire that would

House of Burgesses at Jamestown church by Sidney King, ca. 1957.

eventually carry the English language, laws, and institutions across North America. . . . Representative government, first established at Jamestown in 1619, would in time blossom into a vibrant political culture throughout the British colonies and contribute to a new republican credo expressed in the founding of the United States, which itself would become an inspiration to peoples around the world."

There were, as Horn stressed, many appalling consequences to European colonization, especially its impact on Indians and Africans. Yet, it was at Jamestown, he concluded, that "the peoples of America, Europe, and Africa first encountered one another, lived and worked alongside each other, traded with and fought one another, survived and persisted, and in so doing began the long process—often contentious, sometimes tragic, but ultimately successful—by which together they shaped a new world and forged a new people."

WHAT HAPPENED
AT WILLIAMSBURG

*M*iddle Plantation, as the settlement that became Williamsburg was once known, dates to about 1633 when the area was "laid off and paled in," that is, walled or fortified. Middle Plantation was about halfway between the James and York Rivers, so about five and one-half miles from either side. The settlement was headquarters for Nathaniel Bacon Jr. during Bacon's Rebellion. Other notable events from the early years were the establishment of Bruton Parish in 1674, the completion of a brick church in 1683, and the royal charter for the College of William and Mary in 1693. William and Mary is the second oldest college (after Harvard) in the United States.

Those two institutions, the church and the college, were linked. The Reverend Dr. James Blair served for nearly fifty years as president of William and Mary and thirty-two years as rector of Bruton Parish. The college was intended in part to provide the colony with Church of England clergymen. All the presidents and all except one faculty member during the colonial period were Anglican clergymen. The royal charter for the college came from—no surprise here—King William and Queen Mary.

The third *C* to shape Williamsburg was, of course, the Capitol. After the statehouse at Jamestown burned in 1698, the General Assembly moved the capital to Middle Plantation. It was not an obvious choice to everyone; a couple of decades earlier, when the settlement's boosters put forward the idea of moving the capital there, the king's commissioners replied it made as much sense as if "*London* might have beene new built on *Highgat* Hill, and removed from the grand River that brings them in their Trade."

Before picking Middle Plantation, the General Assembly listened to witnesses, including five students from William and Mary. One student noted that Middle Plantation already had "a Church, an ordinary, several stores, two Mills, a smiths shop a Grammar School, and above all the Colledge." Another spoke of its ideal location as a "wholsome and pleasant" place. "Wholsome" and "pleasant" didn't describe Jamestown. The college students' testimony, however, did not make the difference. The royal governor, Francis Nicholson, was an enthusiastic town planner, having already been at least partly responsible for the plan for Annapolis. Here was another chance to practice his art. The Assembly gave him what he wanted. It voted

to build the new Capitol "somewhere at Middle Plantation nigh his Majesties Royall Colledg of *William* and *Mary*." The new capital was renamed Williamsburg in honor of William III.

The centerpiece of the new town was Duke of Gloucester Street, ninety-nine feet wide and straight between the main building at William and Mary at the west end and the new Capitol at the east, not quite a mile. Duke of Gloucester Street was paralleled by two streets named—are we ready?—Francis to the south, Nicholson to the north.

About halfway down Duke of Gloucester was Market Square. The Governor's Palace was to the north with a view of Duke of Gloucester across a long green. By 1722, when the city was incorporated, a local observer wrote that Williamsburg was "made a Market Town, . . . and is well stock'd with rich Stores, of all Sorts of Goods, and well furnished with the best Provisions and Liquors."

Plenty happened in Williamsburg, but more important than the series of events were the ideas about independence that evolved here. In the first sixty or so years of its existence, Williamsburg was as much a copy of English manners as its inhabitants—artisans, merchants, professionals, and wealthy planters from throughout the region—could afford. Thomas Jefferson would later call it "the finest school of manners and morals that ever existed in America." The people thought of themselves as English, not American. What happened, in the mid-eighteenth century, was that people began to think of the freedom they expected as English. The original idea was not freedom *from* Britain but freedom *in* Britain. The colonists wanted the rights and privileges that other English enjoyed. They did not want to be second-class subjects. That they reached that conclusion while holding slaves is, at least, ironic.

The idea of Americans as a separate people evolved gradually, partly because, though people continued to come to America (indeed, they are still coming), more and more were also born in America. The French and Indian War gave the idea a big push.

The war started when the French, who were in Canada, moved south and claimed the Ohio Valley. Meanwhile, royal officials in Williamsburg were giving land grants in the Ohio Valley. If the French held that land, that would end the westward expansion of the English settlers. George Washington, in 1753 a twenty-one-year-old major in the Virginia militia, was sent to tell the French to get out of there . . . or else. The French declined. A few months later, Washington, now a lieutenant colonel, returned to the region with about 160 men. His troops attacked, killing a French commander before being forced back to Fort Necessity in southwest Pennsylvania. There he was besieged by about 700 men and forced to surrender. It was the first time Washington had commanded troops in action and the only time he would surrender.

Relations between France and Britain worsened, and, in 1756, the war that had already been fought for two years was declared. Indians fought on both sides, but more allied with the French. When the war ended seven years later, the English had won, and the French gave up most of their North American territory, including Canada, east of the Mississippi River.

THE
JOURNAL
OF
Major George Washington,
SENT BY THE
Hon. ROBERT DINWIDDIE, Esq;
His Majesty's Lieutenant-Governor, and
Commander in Chief of VIRGINIA,
TO THE
COMMANDANT
OF THE
FRENCH FORCES
ON
OHIO.
To which are added, the
GOVERNOR's LETTER;
AND A TRANSLATION OF THE
French OFFICER's ANSWER.
WILLIAMSBURG:
Printed by WILLIAM HUNTER. 1754

The French and Indian War may not have been the first time the colonies cooperated, but it was a rare occurrence when all thirteen worked together toward a common goal. It was about this time that some colonists began to refer to themselves as Americans.

What led to the Revolution, more than the French and Indian War itself, was the war's aftermath. The war was expensive. So was guaranteeing the peace on the frontier. The British parliament thought it was not asking too much for colonists to help pay those costs, so it passed the Stamp Act in March 1765. Colonists were required to pay a tax on almost all printed paper they purchased, even playing cards. However, the colonies had no representation in Parliament, and English people had the right to be taxed only by a body in which they had representation, so only the Virginia General Assembly could tax Virginians, or so Virginians said. Other colonies had similar reactions.

This was when Patrick Henry began to make his reputation as a hothead, a Revolutionary, and an orator. In later years, Henry acknowledged that his speaking style was influenced by Samuel Davies, a Presbyterian minister in Hanover County whose sermons Henry had heard during what historians call the Great Awakening. The Great Awakening may also have helped set the tone for the American Revolution. The Great Awakening questioned religious authority, such as that of the Church of England, the state church in Virginia and some other colonies. The Revolution questioned political authority, such as that of the royal governor. Once you begin to question any institution or authority, it's hard to stop. On his twenty-ninth birthday, when Henry had been in the House of Burgesses for only nine days, instead of sitting quietly as a "new boy" was expected to, he proposed and pushed through the Stamp Act resolves, much to the distress of more traditional members.

"If This Be Treason, Make the Most of It!"

The "trumpet of the Revolution" Patrick Henry was called, largely because of a speech he gave in Williamsburg after the British parliament passed the onerous Stamp Act requiring colonists to purchase and affix stamps to various legal and other papers, newspapers, and even playing cards. To Henry, the act trampled on one of the colonists' fundamental rights: that only their elected assemblies could tax them.

"Caesar had his Brutus, Charles the First, his Cromwell, and George the Third may profit by their example," the twenty-nine-year-old Henry exclaimed to the House of Burgesses. From the older, more conservative legislators came cries of "Treason!" to which Henry is said to have responded: "If this be treason, make the most of it."

Stirring words—and they stirred Virginia's burgesses, in May 1765, to pass five resolutions strongly condemning the Stamp Act. Other colonies soon followed suit. A chasm had opened between the colonies and Britain and between Virginia's old gentry and what Gov. Francis Fauquier called the "young hot and giddy" members of the legislature. In a mere decade, there would be revolution.

Despite the fame of his words, there's some doubt as to whether Henry ever spoke them. Many attribute Henry's embrace of treason to William Wirt's 1817 biography. Still, if Henry's actual words have been somewhat mythologized, their effect was not. They did indeed give courage to the fainthearted. In Williamsburg, an angry crowd forced the newly appointed stamp collector to resign. Even moderate leaders like George Washington were soon describing the tax as "a direful attack upon ... Liberties." Various versions of the resolutions, including the one the burgesses rescinded and two others they never passed, found their way into newspapers in other colonies where they spurred defiance of the Stamp Act. Virginia's resolves, wrote Gov. Francis Bernard of Massachusetts, were an "alarm Bell to the disaffected." Americans boycotted British goods, and British merchants pressured Parliament to repeal the tax.

"Scholars may dispute about ... the text of early orations," wrote historian Bernard Mayo. "But [Henry] deserves his fame as 'The Trumpet of the Revolution.' In 1765 on his first days in the House of Burgesses, with his Stamp Act resolves backed by his Treason speech, he ... powerfully stiffened resistance throughout British America."

A Map of the British and French Dominions in North America by John Mitchell, 1755.

What happened in Virginia applied only to Virginia, but Virginia was the largest, most populous, and wealthiest of the thirteen colonies, and newspapers in the other colonies carried reports of what happened here. Virginia was twice the size of the next two largest colonies—Pennsylvania and Massachusetts—combined. In those days, Virginia included what would become Kentucky, West Virginia, and part of Ohio. At the time of the Stamp Act and Henry's resolves, the *Boston Gazette* reported Virginia to be in a state of "utmost consternation." Parliament repealed the Stamp Act but passed the Declaratory Act, which said that it was supreme in the colonies in all cases whatsoever.

For the next ten years, Parliament and the colonies argued. Parliament would pass laws; the colonies would protest them. In 1770, five Americans were shot to death in Boston while protesting the Townshend Acts; three years after that, the Boston Tea Party protested the Tea Act; nine months later, the first Continental Congress met in Philadelphia and asked Americans to boycott everything British.

On April 19, 1775, British troops marched from Boston at night to confiscate American guns at Concord. At Lexington, they were met by a small group of Americans. Someone fired a single shot;

the British fired and killed eight Massachusetts militia, minutemen. The American Revolutionary War, not yet declared, had started. Years later, John Adams put a different date on it: "The Revolution was effected before the war commenced. The Revolution was in the minds and hearts of the people." How did revolution get into the people's minds and hearts? To a large extent, that is what happened in Williamsburg and Virginia.

Williamsburg's population was a fraction of that of Philadelphia or Boston or New York. The town itself probably did not have more than eighteen hundred to two thousand people (about half of whom were slaves), except when the high court was in session. Those "Publick Times" drew people from throughout Virginia and were occasions for partying, gambling, horse racing, and socializing with friends from outside town. (The colony's legislature was sometimes in session at the same time.) To put it another way, during the Revolution, Williamsburg's importance far outweighed its size.

The Boston Tea Party—Destruction of the Tea in Boston Harbor, December 16, 1773, from *Ballou's Pictorial Drawing-Room Companion,* July 26, 1856.

Many of the Revolutionary figures we recognize from Virginia were not townspeople; they lived on plantations, but Williamsburg was the center of their political and intellectual world. Their social life also brought them to town, where they talked to each other, dined and danced together, argued and debated their ideas, allowing these to form, take hold, and spread. In 1760, Thomas Jefferson began to study at the College of William and Mary, and, two years later, he studied law under George Wythe (sounds like "with"). A few years later, Jefferson said that, in Williamsburg, "I have heard more good sense, more rational and philosophical conversations, than in all my life besides."

In September 1771, the new governor, John Murray, fourth Earl of Dunmore, came to Williamsburg after one year as governor of New York. He was the seventh governor to live in Williamsburg, and he seems to have been less reluctant than some of his predecessors to flaunt to the colonists his superior station and to take military action. Those traits helped make him the last royal governor of Virginia.

Two years later, at the Boston Tea Party, Revolutionaries dressed as Mohawks boarded the *Dartmouth*, the *Eleanor*, and the *Beaver;* chopped open 342 chests of tea; and threw the contents into the harbor. Even some of the Revolution's leaders, Benjamin Franklin among them, were appalled by the theft and destruction of private property. Their reaction was nothing compared to Parliament's. It passed the Boston Port Bill of 1774, one of the Coercive Acts. The

bill essentially closed the port of Boston. George III said, "The Colonies must either submit or triumph." He meant for the colonies to submit.

Williamsburg was back in a leadership role with members of the House of Burgesses setting up formal ways of communicating among the colonies and establishing groups that would continue to govern when the official assemblies were dissolved by royal governors. It had taken something as dramatic as London's move to destroy Boston to convince the various colonial leaders that they had to act together. To show solidarity with Boston, Virginia's burgesses set June 1, 1774,

the day the harbor was to be closed, as a day of fasting, humiliation, and prayer in Virginia. Lord Dunmore responded by dissolving the House of Burgesses. The delegates walked down Duke of Gloucester Street to the Raleigh Tavern, met in the Apollo Room, and voted to call a convention to elect delegates to a continental congress in Philadelphia.

Virginia began to change informally from rule by a royal governor to rule by an elected assembly. You cannot put a date on it. People's attitudes changed but not all at once. The Crown, which had ruled since 1624, lost its grip in Virginia although London did not quite grasp what had happened. For that matter, neither did

Virginia. What was happening, though a sea change, had not been recognized because it was gradual and because it was so far outside everyone's experience. "The mysterious rise of American democracy," historian Sean Wilentz wrote, "was an extraordinary part of the most profound political transformation in modern history: the triumph of popular government and of the proposition . . . that sovereignty rightly belongs to the mass of ordinary individual and equal citizens."

Two months after the day of fasting for Boston, Virginia's burgesses picked delegates for the first Continental Congress in Philadelphia and gave those delegates clear instructions: All imports from Great Britain would stop on November 1, and, if the blockade of Boston did not end in one year, all exports to Britain from the colonies would end, including Virginia's own tobacco. The meeting to select and instruct delegates became known as the first Virginia Convention.

The Virginia Convention is also remembered for what it did not do. It did not endorse Thomas Jefferson's *A Summary View of the Rights of British America*, which in strong terms charged George

King George III by Richard Purcell, ca. 1762.

III with a number of civil crimes against the colonists. Jefferson's essay went too far for the majority of the delegates. It was a point-by-point indictment of the king, a format Jefferson would later use in the Declaration of Independence. It was too radical for the 1774 Convention. When the Convention refused to adopt it, *A Summary View* was published as a pamphlet and widely read on both sides of the Atlantic, spreading Jefferson's fame well beyond Virginia. It also clearly demonstrated his ability as a writer. He was not yet thirty-one.

The seven Virginia delegates to Philadelphia were Peyton Randolph, Richard Henry Lee, George Washington, Patrick Henry, Richard Bland, Benjamin Harrison, and Edmund Pendleton. Each was paid half a *johannes* a day. A *johannes* was a Portuguese gold coin worth about three English pounds. Jefferson, sick at home with dysentery, was not in the delegation. His cousin Peyton Randolph, who had enormous experience as Speaker of the House of Burgesses, was elected president of the Continental Congress, making him the first president of a body representing the not-yet United States of America. Randolph died in 1775, the year before independence was declared.

There were fifty-six delegates from twelve colonies attending that first Continental Congress in September 1774. Georgia refused to take part. It was at the Congress that Patrick Henry declared, "I am not a Virginian, but an American." The Virginia delegation got Congress to pass an immediate ban on imports but to hold off for a year on a ban on exports. That let Virginia clear its warehouses of tobacco, an economic necessity. Congress also passed the Suffolk County Resolves, which urged Americans not to pay taxes or trade with Britain and to hold weekly militia

Patrick Henry by Thomas Sully, 1815.

drills—virtually a declaration of war. Congress adjourned in October 1774, and, in November, Revolutionaries threw tea from a merchant ship at Yorktown into the York River: No imports from Britain.

The second Virginia Convention met in Richmond in March 1775. Most delegates, who were as wrong as they could be, thought Britain would give in to avoid a trade embargo and a fight with the colonies. After all, were they not all English? On the third day of the Convention, however, Patrick Henry proposed that the Virginia militia be trained and prepared for war. "I know not what course others may take," Henry supposedly said, "but as for me, give me liberty, or give me death!" One month later, the British army raided Concord and killed minutemen at Lexington along the way.

George Washington by Gilbert Stuart, 1795.

The debate between the king and his colonies became a war with the battles at Lexington and Concord. Two days later, on April 21, 1775, Lord Dunmore sent English seamen to seize the Virginia Colony's gunpowder from the Williamsburg magazine to keep it away from the Revolutionaries. In the various confrontations that followed, Dunmore threatened or hinted that, if Virginians marched on the capital, Dunmore would free the rebels' slaves and arm them. Two months later, Dunmore fled to HMS *Fowey* in the York River.

In May 1775, the second Continental Congress met at Philadelphia to consider what to do about Lexington and Concord. The obvious necessity was to stitch together an army of the separate colonial militias and appoint someone to command it. After the first Continental Congress, when Washington went back to Virginia, several of the colony's militia units elected him to command because of his experience in the French and Indian War. Washington was tall and strong, and he looked and acted like a leader. He rarely spoke in public and seldom took part in debate. Besides, southern colonies had the votes to defeat any other candidate. He was elected commander in chief on the first ballot. Washington turned to his colleague Patrick Henry and said, "Remember, Mr. Henry, what I now tell you: From the day I enter upon the command of the American armies, I date my fall, and the ruin of my reputation." Washington would insist later that he had not wanted command though he was the only delegate to wear his militia uniform to the Congress.

In August 1775, George III declared the colonies in rebellion, and, in November, Dunmore's proclamation freed those Virginia slaves, of rebel masters, who would fight for the British. As a strategic move, freeing the slaves probably was iffy. Some slaves were attracted because the promise of freedom, however remote, was better than nothing. Several hundred eventually joined the British forces. At the same time, Dunmore's proclamation alienated white moderates and those who had not made up their minds. The proclamation also declared martial law in Virginia, which made every able-bodied man who did not rally to the king a traitor who could be executed.

Meanwhile, Virginians continued to prepare for war. The third Virginia Convention met in July and August and ordered the formation of a professional army of two regiments totaling over a thousand men. Some of these soldiers were in Norfolk on New Year's Day 1776 when British ships fired on the city and marines burned part of the town. Some of the American units thought it was the British invasion they had feared, so they set fire to anything that might help the British. It was not a major invasion, but the partial destruction of Norfolk pushed more Virginians and some people in other colonies into the fight for independence.

Continental currency, 1775.

A few days later, colonists in Philadelphia began to buy a newly printed pamphlet called *Common Sense*. It was forty-six pages, and it argued that the colonies must declare independence from "the Royal Brute of Britain." In the first three months, it sold 120,000 copies despite a cover price of two shillings, expensive in those days. George Washington had it read to his troops to make sure that even those who could not read knew what *Common Sense* said. It spread rapidly through the colonies and was excerpted in the *Virginia Gazette* of Williamsburg in February.

It was written by Thomas Paine, who had been in the colonies only fourteen months. Paine was drawn to America from England by a book he had read: "I happened, when a school-boy, to pick up a pleasing natural history of Virginia, and my inclination from that day of seeing the western side of the Atlantic never left me." Paine was not a wealthy man, not well educated, not a lawyer. His writing

Thomas Paine by P. Kramer, 1851.

style was forceful, direct, and understandable by anyone who read or heard it. Paine's biographer Harvey Kaye said Paine was "one of the most remarkable political writers of the modern world and the greatest radical of a radical age." Paine's pamphlet was the first American runaway best seller: it sold at least 500,000 copies. Paine donated the money he made from it to help finance the Revolutionary War.

The military campaign would be in the North for a while, but the idea of rebellion was thriving in Virginia. The fifth and last of the colony's Revolutionary conventions met in the spring and early summer of 1776 in Williamsburg. It instructed Virginia's congressional delegation to introduce a resolution for independence. Richard Henry Lee, in Congress in Philadelphia, accordingly moved, "That these United Colonies are, and of right ought to be, free and independent States, that they are absolved from all allegiance to the British Crown, and that all political connection between them and the State of Great Britain is, and ought to be, totally dissolved." No longer was the goal freedom *in* Britain, now it was freedom *from* Britain.

After it sent instructions to the congressional delegation to move for independence, the Convention adopted the Virginia Declaration of Rights, originally written by George Mason, one of the Revolutionary thinkers who isn't much remembered nowadays.

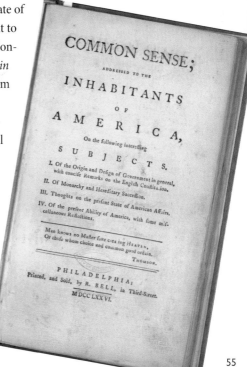

COMMON SENSE;

ADDRESSED TO THE

INHABITANTS

OF

AMERICA,

On the following interesting

SUBJECTS.

I. Of the Origin and Design of Government in general, with concise Remarks on the English Constitution.
II. Of Monarchy and Hereditary Succession.
III. Thoughts on the present State of American Affairs.
IV. Of the present Ability of America, with some miscellaneous Reflections.

Man knows no Master save creating Heaven,
Or those whom choice and common good ordain.
THOMSON.

PHILADELPHIA;
Printed, and Sold, by R. BELL, in Third-Street.
MDCCLXXVI.

The Declaration of Rights

That all men are by nature equally free and independent, and have certain inherent rights, of which, when they enter into a state of society, they cannot, by any compact, deprive or divest their posterity; namely, the enjoyment of life and liberty, with the means of acquiring and possessing property, and pursuing and obtaining happiness and safety.

Sound familiar?

It's not the Declaration of Independence, but Thomas Jefferson certainly drew on this document, Virginia's Declaration of Rights, which was adopted the month before the Declaration of Independence. The primary author of the Virginia Declaration was George Mason. Mason's Declaration also influenced the French Declaration of the Rights of Man and the Citizen, which was to the French Revolution what Jefferson's Declaration of Independence was to the American. Among the principles Mason set forth in the Declaration of Rights were that all power is derived from the people, that people have the right to a trial by jury, and that cruel and unusual punishments ought not to be inflicted. The Declaration also declared freedom of the press and free exercise of religion.

George Mason by Louis Mathieu Didier Guillaume, 1800s.

The Declaration of Rights was the work of the fifth Virginia Convention, which convened in Williamsburg in May 1776. On May 15, the Convention voted to instruct its delegates to the second Continental Congress in Philadelphia to propose independence. The next order of business was to create a new government for Virginia. It was an indication of just how important the Convention considered a citizen's inherent rights that, before getting down to work on a constitution, it first set out to prepare a declaration of rights. To Mason, whose reputation for writing matched Jefferson's, fell the task of writing the first draft.

Mason originally set forth ten points as "the Basis and Foundation of Government," the first being the equality of all men and their natural rights to life, liberty, and property. Immediately, the Convention was faced with the same predicament that later bedeviled Jefferson. Did this universal liberty abolish slavery? How could you guarantee every man's right to property when that property included other men? It was Edmund Pendleton, this time, who found the way around the seemingly absolute language. Pendleton suggested adding the phrase "when they enter into a state of society." Since the delegates all understood that black people could not enter into Virginia society, slaveholders could endorse the Declaration.

On June 12, 1776, after some quick compromising and revising by Mason and others, the Convention adopted the final version of the Declaration of Rights, with sixteen clauses. (Strangely, it was Mason's draft of the Declaration rather than the final approved version that ended up circulating around the colonies and the world, leaving its mark on the French and American Revolutions.) The Convention then moved onto a constitution, which was also written in large part by Mason. It was adopted on June 29.

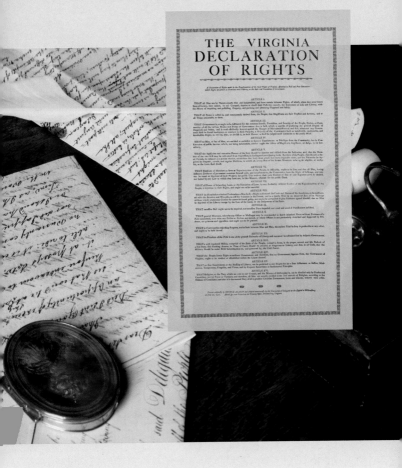

Undeniably, the Declaration of Rights excluded not only slaves but also women. Still, it enumerated many of the rights we now take for granted. Its principles, like those in the Declaration of Independence, set a standard toward which Americans could aspire. "In one sense," wrote historian Josephine Pacheco, "the history of the United States is the effort of excluded groups to claim the Declaration of Rights for themselves, to expand the significance of the ideals that Mason set forth in 1776."

Mason, of course, did not invent the principles in the Declaration. He drew upon British documents, including Magna Carta of 1215, the Petition of Right of 1628, the Habeas Corpus Act of 1679, the Bill of Rights of 1689, and the Act of Settlement of 1701. Colonial charters and practice also influenced his work, as did the writings of political philosophers such as John Locke. But, it was Mason who merged the British and colonial traditions into a single document that became a model for other states and nations. Jefferson, who understood his debt to Mason, described him as "a man of the first order of wisdom among those who acted on the theatre of the revolution, of expansive mind, profound judgment, cogent in argument, learned in the lore of our former constitution, and earnest for the republican change on democratic principles."

Why, then, is Mason such an obscure figure? Partly that's because, although he served in the colonial House of Burgesses, unlike such fellow Virginians as Washington, Jefferson, and Madison, he never sought or attained national office. Indeed, his major foray into national politics was as an anti-Federalist, politicking against adoption of the United States Constitution. Mason objected to the lack of a bill of rights along the lines of those proclaimed in his Declaration. That a bill of rights was ultimately adopted as the first ten amendments to the Constitution is another reason to give Mason a prominent place among the Founding Fathers.

The Declaration of Rights declared free exercise of religion and of the press, and it gave the people the right to a jury trial. It was a model for the U. S. Bill of Rights, the first ten amendments to the U. S. Constitution. The fifth Convention also adopted the first Virginia Constitution, which gave the bulk of the power to the General Assembly, which included an elected house of delegates and senate, while weakening the office of the governor. The goal was to prevent any recurrence of Virginia's experience with a governor like Dunmore. The General Assembly elected Patrick Henry as the first governor of an independent Virginia.

Henry served as governor for three one-year terms. He was succeeded by Jefferson, who served two. Jefferson was governor in 1780 when the capital was moved from Williamsburg to Richmond. Ships' cannons could fire on Williamsburg from either the James or York; Richmond seemed a safer place. It was also more centrally located, given the westward movement of settlers.

In Philadelphia in 1776, one of the results of Richard Henry Lee's proposal was the appointment of a congressional committee of five to draft a declaration of independence. Jefferson was to do the

Thomas Jefferson by Gilbert Stuart, 1805.

original work. He finished in seventeen days using forms and arguments he had used earlier in Virginia. Of the committee, only John Adams and Benjamin Franklin had suggestions, and Jefferson incorporated those and presented the draft to Congress. "Jefferson was proud of his draft," his biographer R. B. Bernstein wrote, "but Congress's response to it caused him enduring pain. . . . Jefferson took each cut and change as a personal affront."

Still, the words came through loud and clear: "We hold these truths to be self-evident, that all men are created equal, that they are endowed by their Creator with certain unalienable Rights, that among these are Life, Liberty and the pursuit of Happiness. That to secure these rights, Governments are instituted among Men, deriving their just powers from the consent of the governed."

Lee's motion to declare independence was approved July 2, 1776, and the Declaration of Independence two days later.

When Richard Henry Lee moved to declare independence, he also moved to form a confederacy of the thirteen colonies. The Articles of Confederation eventually were ratified, but the confederation didn't always work smoothly, especially for the armed forces, because each independent state believed it did not have to do anything it did not want to do. Great for independence; impossible for unity. Democracy then, as now, was an unfinished business. Still, what Virginians, and other Americans, had done was to throw off the chains of monarchy. No longer subjects, they were now citizens.

Richard Henry Lee by Charles Willson Peale, ca. 1795–1805.

Meanwhile, in the field, Washington was fighting the war. For a long time, what he had to do militarily was keep his army in the field. He did not have to win anything; he had to avoid being defeated. American military prospects improved in 1777 when, after British forces surrendered at Saratoga in New York, the French prepared to openly enter the war on the American side.

Before Gen. Charles Cornwallis came to Virginia in 1781, there were raids, battles, and occupations in Williamsburg and elsewhere in Virginia. In April 1781, British troops under Generals William Phillips and Benedict Arnold captured Williamsburg. Arnold had played a crucial role in the American victory at Saratoga but then turned traitor.

In June 1781, Cornwallis occupied Williamsburg, setting up his headquarters at the president's house at the college. His troops spread smallpox, freed slaves, and confiscated supplies. After ten days, Cornwallis moved to Portsmouth before eventually setting up camp at Yorktown. His troops left behind incredible numbers of flies in a day when there was no such thing as insecticide. St. George Tucker, a prominent Williamsburg Revolutionary and lawyer, celebrated the arrival of American troops in Williamsburg telling his wife that Washington was their "Deliverer" and "the Savior of their Country." At Yorktown, Cornwallis would meet the Americans and their French allies. The story now moves from thoughts and ideas in Williamsburg to armies and cannons at Yorktown.

George Washington by
Charles Willson Peale, 1780.

WHAT HAPPENED AT YORKTOWN

The short version of Yorktown goes like this: The British general Lord Charles Cornwallis was in the Carolinas fighting Continental forces. Gen. George Washington was in New York and New Jersey fighting British and German auxiliary forces. They both went to Yorktown, fought, and Washington won the decisive victory of the Revolutionary War. Hurray! (Unless, of course, you are British. Sorry.) While that is accurate, it isn't enough. Washington could not have won without French army and navy units, and there are some good stories that aren't widely known and some people worth meeting who haven't been widely met.

By 1781, Virginia was in trouble. In early January, Benedict Arnold attacked Richmond, burning buildings and destroying public records before withdrawing. It would have been worse, but, after the attack, because of a letter from Gov. Thomas Jefferson asking George Washington to come home and defend his native state, Washington sent the marquis de Lafayette with twelve hundred troops to counter the British forces in Virginia. They arrived in time to stave off another British offensive in April 1781.

Gilbert du Motier, the marquis de Lafayette, was one of the romantic figures of the Revolutionary War. France formally allied with the colonies in 1778, but Lafayette had come the year before entirely on his own. He sailed to the colonies from France, was commissioned a major general by Congress, met Washington in Philadelphia four days later, and joined Washington's staff. Lafayette was, at that time, one month short of his twentieth birthday. He fought well in combat and was wounded. When he was offered a command, he asked for a Virginia division, probably to flatter or honor Washington. He was not dashing. Contemporaries described him as boyish, chubby, ungainly, socially awkward, with already-thinning red hair. It was said that the queen of France collapsed in laughter watching him try to dance. He was married to a woman whose dowry, along with his family fortune, made him one of the richer men in France. George Washington referred to him as a son.

The job he had to do in Virginia seemed impossible. He was, at first, supposed to drive English raiding parties out of the state. Later, when Cornwallis moved his troops from Carolina to Petersburg, Lafayette was ordered to keep Cornwallis in Virginia. The English had

The marquis de Lafayette by Noel Le Mire, 1775–1800.

four times the number of men and an excellently mounted force (on stolen Virginia Thoroughbreds) that could move quickly. The young Frenchman correctly concluded, "I am not strong enough even to get beaten." What to do? "I am therefore determined to skarmish, but not to engage too far." Lafayette had to avoid a pitched battle, which he would lose, keep his troops on the move, run while appearing to give chase, and be the greatest pest to Cornwallis he could possibly be. But, Lafayette could do that only to the extent that he knew where Cornwallis would be and what he planned to do, and, for that, Lafayette needed intelligence. That's where James Armistead came in.

Armistead was a slave from New Kent County, who, with the permission of his owner, William Armistead, became a spy for the Revolution. He joined the British forces in Richmond, became a waiter in the British officers' mess, and stayed with the British until they surrendered at Yorktown, all the while feeding information to Lafayette. He was a master spy, setting up reporting systems and so ingratiating himself with Cornwallis that the British general asked Armistead to spy for *him*. Armistead could then easily report information to the Continentals and misinformation to the British. Of course, there are few records—spies do not usually keep written records—so what was learned from the spy system is a matter of conjecture. Whatever it was, it had to be a comfort to the Continentals to know that much of what was discussed in the British officers' mess at dinner was reported to Lafayette before breakfast. (At the end of the war, Armistead returned to slavery, but, when Lafayette came back to Virginia in 1784, he wrote a special testimonial on Armistead's behalf to the Virginia General Assembly. Armistead won his freedom in 1787 and changed his named to James Armistead Lafayette.)

Charles Cornwallis by Benjamin Smith, 1798.

In the field, Lafayette was reinforced with Pennsylvanians. Cornwallis stopped trying to seize all of Virginia and moved toward Williamsburg, which he reached June 25. On July 6, Cornwallis's forces battled Lafayette's at Green Spring near Jamestown. It was the largest open-field engagement in Virginia. Cornwallis inflicted heavy casualties on the Americans. Cornwallis then crossed the James River, taking his army to Portsmouth. During the first week of August, wanting a defensible position near the Chesapeake Bay, Cornwallis moved his troops to Yorktown. Lafayette was reporting every British movement in detail to General Washington, which was almost certainly the work of Armistead and his waiter spies.

By the end of August, the French admiral the comte de Grasse had arrived in the Chesapeake Bay from the West Indies with somewhere between three and four thousand French troops. At the same time, a British fleet under Adm. Thomas Graves sailed from New York. The battle at sea started after four o'clock in the afternoon of September 5, 1781. Graves had nineteen ships and fourteen hundred guns; de Grasse had five more ships, three hundred more guns. It was the largest naval battle of the Revolutionary War. When the fighting stopped that night, there were about 336 British sailors killed or wounded and about 220 French.

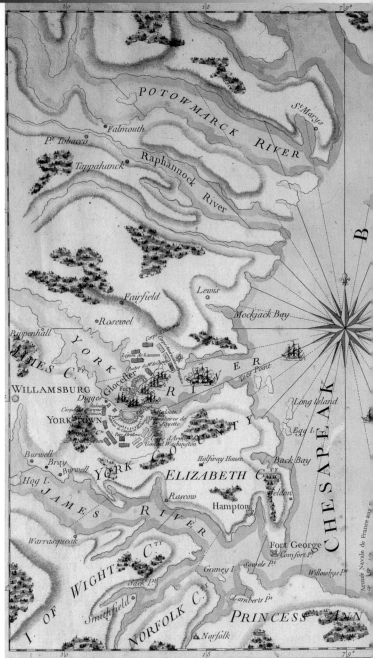

Carte de la Partie de la Virginie, maker unknown, 1781.

The ships drifted a hundred miles from the Chesapeake Bay without another battle but keeping an eye on each other. On September 9, de Grasse slipped away and headed back to the bay. There he found Adm. Louis de Barras, who had sailed eight more French fighting vessels from Rhode Island. He also brought French siege guns and salted meat for the troops. By the time Graves got back, he

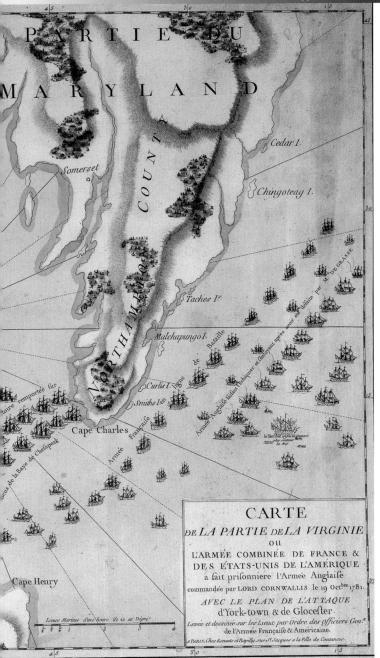

CARTE
DE LA PARTIE DE LA VIRGINIE
OU
L'ARMÉE COMBINÉE DE FRANCE &
DES ÉTATS-UNIS DE L'AMÉRIQUE
a fait prisonniere l'Armée Angloise
commandée par LORD CORNWALLIS le 19 Oct.bre 1781.
AVEC LE PLAN DE L'ATTAQUE
d'York-town & de Glocester.
Levée et dessinée sur les Lieux par Ordre des Officiers Gen.x
de l'Armée Françoise & Americaine.
A PARIS, Chez Esnauts et Rapilly, rue St. Jacques a la Ville de Coutances.

was hopelessly outgunned, so he headed to New York to repair and refit his fleet. By September 10, the Chesapeake Bay was a French pond. The upshot was that Cornwallis could not escape by sea.

While the two fleets battled on September 5, George Washington was en route to Virginia with twenty-five hundred Continentals and a French army under the command of the comte de Rochambeau, who had arrived in Rhode Island the summer before with fifty-five hundred soldiers. Meanwhile, Cornwallis continued to dig in. His orders were to hold a deepwater port.

Yorktown had once been the busiest tobacco port on the Chesapeake, but that had passed thirty years before. In 1750, the population of Yorktown was between five and eight hundred; the town was never larger. As tobacco wore the land out and plantations moved inland, new ports were built upriver on the York and the James. In its heyday, a visiting Englishman wrote of Yorktown, "You perceive a great Air of Opulence amongst the Inhabitants." He described "Houses, equal in Magnificence to many of our superb ones at St. James's." A few fine brick homes still stood on the bluff above the town. The street next to the river had wharves and warehouses to serve the port and hovels and bars to serve the workers. The "great Air of Opulence" was gone. When the English and Germans moved into town, a unit of three hundred Virginia militia slipped away, and only a few civilians remained.

A brief aside. After Washington and Rochambeau arrived in Williamsburg, they were taken to the *Ville de Paris*, de Grasse's flagship in the bay, to greet the admiral and make sure his fleet

stayed around. De Grasse was six foot two, and his sailors swore that, during combat, he grew four inches. Washington was a big and powerful man, even taller than de Grasse. One can only wonder how Washington felt, according to a story passed down by his family, when de Grasse pulled himself to his full Gallic height, stretched up to kiss Washington on both cheeks, and welcomed him with the words "*Mon cher petit général* [My dear little general]!"

With de Grasse's fleet anchored in Hampton Roads, French transports moved up the James River. The night of September 2, thirty-two hundred French troops came ashore at Jamestown by torchlight in clouds of mosquitoes. Lafayette now had fifty-five hundred regulars and three thousand militia. On September 26, the main allied force under Washington and Rochambeau assembled at Williamsburg. By the time the siege started, the Continentals and French outnumbered the British and Germans by roughly two to one.

Also present at the siege were a number of black soldiers from a Rhode Island unit composed largely of former slaves. All told, probably about eight thousand African Americans served in the Continental army during the Revolution. Many returned to slavery after the war.

Washington and His Generals at Yorktown by James Peale, 1781–1790.

Before modern communications, the fife and drum corps gave signals to armies, usually by drums, whose beat could be heard

at a distance. No one in Washington's camp was surprised when, on the morning of September 28, 1781, drums sounded the beat to march. The next day the allied armies moved into position around Yorktown. The Americans and French maneuvered closer to Yorktown, bringing up their cannons and siege guns amidst sporadic shots from British cannons and howitzers. The allies dug trenches and built cannon batteries.

By October 9, the first artillery batteries were ready. At about three o'clock in the afternoon, the French opened fire. Two hours later, at the end of an afternoon of brilliant sunshine, the American battery opened fire. Dr. James Thacher, a young surgeon at Yorktown, wrote in his diary, "His Excellency General Washington put the match to the first gun, and a furious discharge of cannon and mortars immediately followed." The French and American guns had great precision, putting an end to Lord Cornwallis's hope that the enemy had no heavy artillery.

Once the cannonade started, it did not stop. A German soldier fighting for the British described the constant bombardment: "The inhabitants of the city fled with their belongings to the water at the river and hid themselves on the hillside in sand and rocks. Still they did not entirely escape." The gun batteries concentrated on the British defensive trenches. There was one break on October 10 at about noon when a white flag appeared on the British parapet and two soldiers escorted an elderly man and his servant to the Continental lines. He was Thomas Nelson, who, prior to the Revolution, had been the colony's secretary. Although he was a patriot, he didn't take an active part in the revolt. The cannonade had severely damaged his home, which Cornwallis used as his headquarters, so the English general had sent the old man to safety. Cornwallis, Nelson reported, now lived in a cave beneath his garden. And, he said, the town was being destroyed.

Nelson's nephew, Thomas Nelson Jr., a signer of the Declaration of Independence and the third governor of Virginia, was with the Continental army that day as brigadier general in command of the Virginia militia. Lafayette had a new battery ready to open fire, so he asked Governor Nelson for a target in Yorktown, a town the governor knew well. Nelson picked a tall, brick house with a large chimney on each end and told Lafayette to aim there. According to a Frenchman present at the scene, Nelson said, "True, it is my house; but, my friends, it is full of English. Do not spare it." The Frenchman continued, "He did not have to tell us twice," and added that it was damaged "beyond repair." In fact, Nelson's home, though struck repeatedly, survived. It's possible that the Frenchman confused the governor's home with that of his uncle, which was damaged beyond repair. Some historians have doubted the story, but there's no reason to doubt the governor's self-sacrificing patriotism.

Yorktown as a whole did not fare well. From October 9 to October 17, American and French shells rained on Yorktown, and the town was as devastated as the British trenches. After the siege, Baron von Closen, an aide to Rochambeau, wrote, "One could not take three steps without running into some great holes made by bombs."

Houses standing were riddled with shot, windowpanes blown out. About 80 percent of the town was destroyed or too badly damaged to be rebuilt. Dr. Thacher added that Yorktown "contains about sixty houses . . . many of them are greatly damaged and some totally ruined, being shot through in a thousand places and honey-combed ready to crumble to pieces." Both men described bodies and parts of bodies in the streets or ditches. Pennsylvania lieutenant Ebenezer Denny was brief: "Never was in so filthy a place."

Until October 14, most of the damage around Yorktown had been done by big guns. That night, for the first time, the infantry

moved to the forefront when a French force and a Continental one, each with about four hundred men, attacked two advanced British positions, known as Redoubts No. 9 and No. 10. The French and Continentals won both positions, but not easily and not without casualties. Leading the charge on Redoubt No. 10 was Lt. Col. Alexander Hamilton from New York.

After he lost the two redoubts, Cornwallis wrote to his commander in New York, "My Situation now becomes very critical. . . . we shall soon be exposed to an Assult in ruined Works, in a bad Position and with weakened Numbers." He fought back as best he could.

In the early morning hours of October 16, with Continentals and French exhausted from the attacks on the redoubts the night before, a British raiding party attacked the line where the Continentals and French joined. It was a bold raid, but it failed to silence the allied guns.

Late that night, Cornwallis tried to get his army across the York River to Gloucester Point. He collected all the small crafts on the banks of the York that had not been damaged by the bombardment. That amounted to only sixteen boats, so his plan was to send his troops across in three waves. His elite troops would go in the first wave in case they had to fight their way out. He would go in the second wave with more troops, leaving a letter to George Washington asking mercy for his sick and wounded, who would be left behind. The first wave got across with no difficulty. Then a storm hit. The boats had just returned from the north bank when a squall came with a ferocity that Tidewater residents know well, scattering the boats, whipping the river into whitecaps, and making travel impossible. The allied force was quiet that night, but Banastre Tarleton, a British officer known as "Bloody Ban" for his massacre of American troops who'd surrendered to him, wrote in his diary, "Thus expired the last hope of the British army."

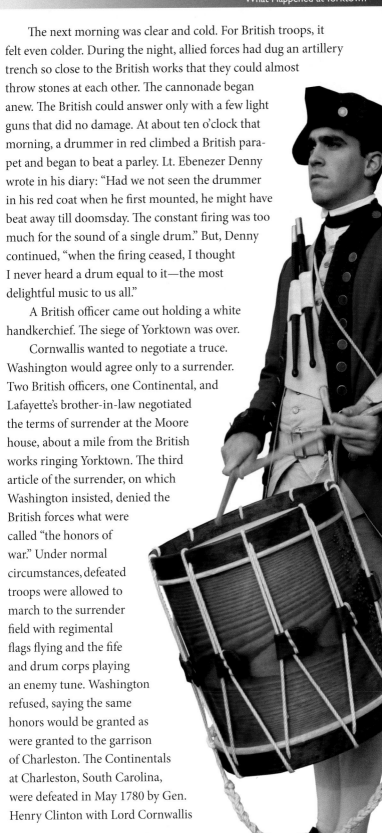

The next morning was clear and cold. For British troops, it felt even colder. During the night, allied forces had dug an artillery trench so close to the British works that they could almost throw stones at each other. The cannonade began anew. The British could answer only with a few light guns that did no damage. At about ten o'clock that morning, a drummer in red climbed a British parapet and began to beat a parley. Lt. Ebenezer Denny wrote in his diary: "Had we not seen the drummer in his red coat when he first mounted, he might have beat away till doomsday. The constant firing was too much for the sound of a single drum." But, Denny continued, "when the firing ceased, I thought I never heard a drum equal to it—the most delightful music to us all."

A British officer came out holding a white handkerchief. The siege of Yorktown was over.

Cornwallis wanted to negotiate a truce. Washington would agree only to a surrender. Two British officers, one Continental, and Lafayette's brother-in-law negotiated the terms of surrender at the Moore house, about a mile from the British works ringing Yorktown. The third article of the surrender, on which Washington insisted, denied the British forces what were called "the honors of war." Under normal circumstances, defeated troops were allowed to march to the surrender field with regimental flags flying and the fife and drum corps playing an enemy tune. Washington refused, saying the same honors would be granted as were granted to the garrison of Charleston. The Continentals at Charleston, South Carolina, were defeated in May 1780 by Gen. Henry Clinton with Lord Cornwallis

Yorktown: The Surrender of Cornwallis published by Mondhare & Jean, ca. 1781.

as second-in-command. The defeated Continental force was granted no honors, so neither was Cornwallis at Yorktown seventeen months later. The defeated Continental commander at Charleston was Maj. Gen. Benjamin Lincoln, now Washington's second-in-command at Yorktown. Once Washington approved the terms, he signed them without ceremony, adding the line, "Done in the Trenches before Yorktown, in Virginia, October 19th, 1781."

The British forces marched to the surrender field led by Gen. Charles O'Hara, Cornwallis's second-in-command. Where was Cornwallis? Sick, he claimed, though many later assumed he was trying to avoid the humiliation of the surrender ceremony. O'Hara headed toward Rochambeau, clearly an effort to avoid surrendering directly to the Americans. Rochambeau's aide pointed to Washington. O'Hara approached Washington and held out his sword. Washington refused the sword and the surrender. If Cornwallis was going to send a subordinate to surrender, protocol demanded that Washington send

a subordinate to accept it. Lincoln took O'Hara's sword.

There were reports that many of the British were drunk. About thirty-five hundred troops stacked their arms and marched away between lines of French and Continentals. Another thirty-five hundred troops, mostly sick and wounded, waited in the trenches. Most of the British officers, by the custom of the day, were "paroled." Most, including Cornwallis, eventually returned to England. He later became governor-general of India and viceroy of Ireland. The rank and file were marched to American prison camps in Virginia and Maryland where they awaited negotiations that would free them.

Among those who fared worst were the thousands of slaves who fled to what they hoped would be freedom under the British. After the surrender at Yorktown, there were reports of "herds of Negroes" fleeing through Virginia's swamps and woods. Hundreds of Cornwallis's former soldiers were captured by their former owners.

The World Turned Upside Down

According to an oft-told tale, as the British troops marched out to surrender at Yorktown on October 19, 1781, their musicians played a tune called "The World Turned Upside Down." "If summer were spring," the lyrics went, "then all the world would be upside down!"

Other lyrics had also been set to the same music, including a ballad known as "The King Enjoys His Own Again." The king would not have enjoyed his troops' surrender, and those words were clearly inappropriate. In contrast, what could have been more appropriate than the words to "The World Turned Upside Down"?

This is a nice story, one told in various forms by such esteemed historians as Samuel Eliot Morison and Richard Ketchum. It is almost as good a story as George Washington's cherry tree. And, according to some historians, it is just as untrue.

For one thing, the British were hardly in the mood to be playful about their choice of music. As they marched between the French and American victors, many on both sides recalled, the British refused even to look at the Americans. Cornwallis himself avoided the ignominy of surrender by sending his second-in-command, Brig. Gen. Charles O'Hara. Many of the surrendering redcoats appeared to be drunk, perhaps having emptied their bottles of rum to steel themselves for the ceremony.

Moreover, in all the accounts from the period—and the surrender was widely reported in newspapers, letters, and journals—there's no mention of "The World Turned Upside Down." The accounts mention that music was played and that there was a peculiar strain of melancholy, but nothing more specific. The story that it was "The World Turned Upside Down" didn't appear in print until 1828 in Alexander Garden's *Anecdotes of the American Revolution*. Music historian Arthur Schrader dismissed the story as a "sound bite."

All of which is not to deny that the surrender at Yorktown turned the world upside down. "The opportunity to combine his land forces with French naval power to enclose Cornwallis in the vulnerable position he had chosen at Yorktown would be, Washington realized, his one chance to defeat the enemy and bring a culmination to the long struggle," wrote historian Barbara Tuchman. "The junction in Virginia had to be coordinated by two different national commands separated across an ocean without benefit of telephone, telegraph or wireless. That this was carried out without a fault seems accountable only by a series of miracles."

For those who insist that such a story be accompanied by music, take heart. Even if the British never played "The World Turned Upside Down," there are many reports that the Americans at Yorktown had their own fifes and drums. The tune they played was "Yankee Doodle."

Le Temple de la Gloire. Capitulation de Cornwallis by Jean Louis Delignon, 1782–1800.

Everyone on the British side had hoped for rescue or resupply from New York. The failure to rescue or resupply Cornwallis should stand as a textbook example of how not to conduct a military campaign. In New York, during the month or so before the surrender, the British held thirteen high-ranking councils of war. Nothing was decided, or what was decided was changed at the next council. Graves did not send his damaged ships to be repaired for four days, and then more time was lost looking for lumber to repair them. Several more days went by while everyone in New York entertained sixteen-year-old Prince William Henry, the future William IV, who had arrived from London. The biggest reasons for delay were that Gen. Henry Clinton, Cornwallis's superior, could not accept how bad the news from Cornwallis actually was, and Graves did not want to face the French ships in Virginia again. The one person at headquarters who insisted that something be done right away was naval captain William Cornwallis, the earl's younger brother. He was ignored. Finally, the same day the English drummer beat parley, the first couple of ships put to sea, and, the day Cornwallis's troops laid down their arms, the rescue fleet sailed. It arrived five days later, just as most of the British troops were led off to prison camps.

In London, most of the blame fell on Gen. Henry Clinton. Clinton blamed everyone who was remotely involved, and, once back in England, he wrote a reconstruction of the war that blamed the king's cabinet and the English generals, especially Cornwallis. No one

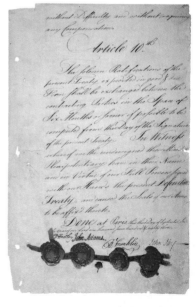

Treaty of Paris.

seemed to care. In London, Lord North was driven from the prime minister's office, George III wrote a letter of abdication to Parliament but never sent it, and retired merchant Richard Osborne was named to open peace negotiations with the Americans.

The victory at Yorktown was decisive but not final. The war continued, and people died in battles that had no real significance. By the spring of 1782, fighting east of the Appalachian Mountains had pretty much stopped. The war formally ended with the Treaty of Paris in 1783. John Jay, one of the American negotiators, wrote in his diary, "If we are not a happy people now it will be our own fault."

When the war ended, there were thirteen independent entities. There was still no United States. In 1783, Congress had nothing beyond begging rights. The sovereign states did not keep their promises, did not levy continental taxes, did not send men to the armed forces. Thomas Jefferson imagined the states going to war with each other and inviting European allies into the country. Washington sounded even more bitter: "What a triumph for the advocates of despotism to find that we are incapable of governing ourselves, and that systems founded on the basis of equal liberty are merely ideal and fallacious!"

The American Revolution turned us from subjects to citizens. The nature of that citizenship was—and still is—evolving. The next step was the Constitution. "In 1787, democratic self-government existed almost nowhere on earth," the Constitutional scholar Akhil Reed Amar wrote. "America's Founding gave the world more democracy than the planet had thus far witnessed."

By June 1788, nine states ratified the Constitution. Washington was sworn in as president in 1789, not quite eight full years after Yorktown.

It took 174 years to travel across the peninsula from Jamestown to Yorktown. It actually was a great deal further. What started at Jamestown came to fruition at Williamsburg and then Yorktown. The story of Virginia's Historic Triangle is the story of America's quest for freedom—a quest that continues today.

Visiting Jamestown

Introducing Jamestown

*J*amestown would be easier to explain if it were one place, but it isn't. Jamestown is two places, and both are crucial to understanding the first permanent English-speaking settlement in the New World. There's Historic Jamestowne (with a final silent *e*), the actual site of the original colony, and Jamestown Settlement, a living history museum that tells the story of the people who lived there. How did that come about?

When the capital moved to Williamsburg in 1699, Jamestown began to deteriorate. By 1616, Jamestown had a church, a courthouse, and a few brick houses, but, after 1699, the area became farmland. There might still be nothing to see at Jamestown were it not for the efforts of Preservation Virginia, the nation's first statewide preservation organization. Preservation Virginia was founded as the Association for the Preservation of Virginia Antiquities (APVA) in 1889 to save Jamestown.

There is a plaque behind the church on the island that says, "In lasting gratitude to Mr. and Mrs. Edward E. Barney for the gift of this Historic Ground. May 3, 1893." The Barneys gave 22.5 acres of farmland to the APVA, and that was the start of the preservation. The National Park Service acquired the remaining 1,500 or so acres of the island in 1934.

Archaeological excavations on the island started in 1901, and major excavations were conducted in the 1930s and 1950s. Still, for some visitors, all this archaeological activity didn't give a real sense of what life was like in 1607.

So, for the 350th anniversary in 1957, the Commonwealth of Virginia decided to build Jamestown Festival Park, not on Jamestown Island but on land adjacent to the island donated by the National Park Service. The Jamestown-Yorktown Foundation eventually built a re-created Jamestown fort and a typical Powhatan Indian village for visitors to walk through. Life-size replicas of the *Susan Constant,* the *Godspeed,* and the *Discovery* rode at anchor beside a pier. In 1990, Jamestown Festival Park was renamed Jamestown Settlement. For 2007 and the decades beyond, Jamestown Settlement added a 143,000-square-foot exhibition and education complex with a theater, exhibits, a gift shop, and a café.

Meanwhile, the island itself, jointly operated by the National Park Service and Preservation Virginia, became much more of a draw with new discoveries and a new visitor center, archaeological museum, museum store, and café. Archaeological work continues at Historic Jamestowne and more is being learned about our nation's birthplace almost on a daily basis. For years, most believed that the site of Jamestown's fort had been lost to the shifting tides of the James River. In 1994, the original site, except for one corner where the ground has washed away, was found near the old church. The discovery of James Fort by Dr. William Kelso and his Jamestown Rediscovery team was one of the greatest archaeological discoveries of our time. Now we know the specific piece of ground where the colonists first settled in 1607. This is where John Smith took command and where the United States began to take shape.

Excavation and conservation of a fifteenth-century breastplate found at Jamestown fort.

Anniversary Commemorations

1807   For the two hundredth, many Revolutionary War veterans found their way to the area by traveling over rough roads and through wilderness. Festivities included a regatta of sailing vessels, a parade, and speeches by William and Mary students.

1857   Visitors came by ships and steamers to see a military parade and hear a speech by former President John Tyler.

1907   An exposition at what is now the Norfolk naval base was sort of a world's fair with exhibits about the history and culture of other states and countries as well as Virginia. Some states built halls that were replicas of their famous buildings. On Jamestown Island itself, the Tercentenary Monument and Memorial Church were constructed.

1957   The Jamestown Festival attracted Queen Elizabeth II as well as other dignitaries. The celebration's lasting legacies include Jamestown Festival Park, now known as Jamestown Settlement, and the Colonial Parkway, connecting all three points of the Historic Triangle.

2007   Queen Elizabeth returned in May, once again focusing international attention on Jamestown. At Historic Jamestowne, new facilities included the Visitor Center and the Voorhees Archaearium. At Jamestown Settlement, new galleries opened, emphasizing the interactions of the three cultures that converged there; a special exhibit placed Jamestown in its global context. Other highlights included sails of the newly commissioned replica of the *Godspeed* along the East Coast, Virginia Indian heritage events, the national webcast "Jamestown Live!", the State of the Black Union conference, the American Indian Intertribal Cultural Festival, the Virginia Black Expo, and the World Forum on the Future of Democracy.

CAPTAIN
JOHN SMITH
GOVERNOR OF
VIRGINIA
1608

What to See at Historic Jamestowne

www.historicjamestowne.org or www.nps.gov/colo
757-898-3400

*W*hen you drive across the land bridge onto Jamestown Island, you are where the settlers arrived. Much of the island retains the lush, natural setting found by the settlers in 1607. A driving tour around the island gives a clear sense of the swampy wilderness they originally encountered.

In the area of the actual settlement, there was more new construction for Jamestown's four hundredth anniversary than at any time since the seventeenth century. There's the Visitor Center, the Voorhees Archaearium (which interprets how archaeologists found the site of the 1607 James Fort and displays hundreds of the artifacts excavated here), and the remodeled Dale House, originally built in 1912 and now serving food for those facing their own personal "starving time." The new construction makes your visit more comfortable, more convenient, and more informative.

Visitor Center

At the Visitor Center, built for the four hundredth anniversary, an audiovisual presentation, museum exhibits, and a variety of tours and programs provide the background needed to make your visit more meaningful. A sound and light "immersion experience" captures the moods and legacies of Jamestown in a theater-in-the-round setting. The museum gallery presents the entire ninety-two-year history of Jamestown as the capital of Virginia and introduces Jamestown as the place where the people of three continents, North America, Europe, and Africa, first came together.

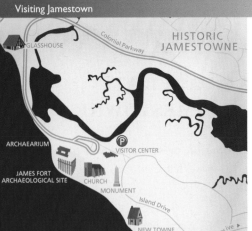

Check at the information desk for the day's schedule of guided tours. Park rangers conduct several tours each day through the original fort and town site, exploring a wide variety of themes related to the history of Jamestown. In the summer months, you may also have as your tour guide one of the early Jamestown settlers: John Rolfe might speak on introducing tobacco to the colony, or Rachel Stanton might recount the arrival of the "bride ships" bringing the first women to the colony.

Leaving the Visitor Center, take the footbridge across a pitch and tar swamp to the fort and town site. At the end of the bridge, directly in front of you is the granite Tercentenary Monument, erected in 1907 to mark the three hundredth anniversary of the founding of Jamestown. To the right is the site of the 1607 James Fort; to the left is New Towne, where the capital of Virginia expanded outside the fort walls starting in the 1620s. To continue your visit, turn to the right and head for the brick church and tower.

CHURCH

The church tower, which dates back to the 1680s, is the only aboveground seventeenth-century structure on the island. The brick Jamestown Memorial Church was built for the 1907 tercentennial.

The first church at Jamestown was little more than a sail tied between trees as an awning with stumps and planks for pews. A few months after arriving, the settlers built a wooden church inside James Fort. In 1617, a new church was built. It was here on July 30, 1619, that the first legislative assembly took place in English North America with elected representatives arriving from each plantation. The 1907 church was built on the foundations of the 1617 frame church, the foundations of which are still visible inside the Memorial Church.

Roots of Democracy

The first representative legislature in Britain's New World, the General Assembly of 1619, was more a product of circumstance than political philosophy.

With the colony failing, the Virginia Company in London was desperately looking for ways to salvage the situation. Company treasurer Sir Edwin Sandys proposed a series of remedies, including granting private ownership of land and authorizing the governor to convene an assembly with "free power, to treat Consult & conclude ... all emergent occasions concerning the pupliqe weale of the said colony."

Sandys did not have in mind an American parliament, let alone a new way of thinking about government. He hoped merely to find a more efficient way to manage a distant colony and to encourage investment and immigration. Royal charters of 1609 and 1612 had given additional power to the governor and his advisory council in Virginia, and Sandys's proposal was an extension of that.

Wrote historian Warren Billings: "An ocean between Jamestown and London, the desire to find private gain in a place largely innocent of European restraints, the need for ways to raise revenue, to improve courts, to delineate parishes, to establish property rights, to settle debts, to correct miscreants, to define matters of race and gender, or to defend the colony—all these ... afforded an ample atmosphere for experimenting with the forms of governance and the uses of power."

So experiment they did.

Gov. George Yeardley and twenty-two elected burgesses met for the first time on July 30, 1619. John Pory, as Speaker of the General Assembly and the colony's secretary, kept a journal. "The most convenient place we could finde to sitt in was the Quire of the Churche," Pory wrote. There the Assembly proposed amendments to the charter, passed laws on tobacco prices and servant contracts, and recommended ways to maintain peace with the Powhatans. They ejected two of their numbers, thus establishing a precedent that the Assembly itself could judge its members' credentials. The Assembly also judged several criminal cases.

In the next few years, the Assembly increased its power, establishing its right to tax colonists and precluding members from arrest during sessions.

The future of the General Assembly was thrown into doubt in 1624 when the Virginia Company collapsed and King James I took direct control of the colony. A year later, King Charles I declared the colony a royal dominion. His proclamation said nothing about the Assembly. This was better than abolishing it, but it was hardly a resounding endorsement.

Fortunately for those who believed in self-government, Virginia's governors saw the General Assembly as a useful aid and continued to call regular sessions. In 1639, Charles gave his official sanction, giving orders for the Assembly to convene annually. Self-government, planted at Jamestown in 1619, was now firmly rooted in American soil.

Jamestown Rediscovery excavations, 1996.

Fort

If you stand in the tower door and look straight ahead, you are looking at the site of James Fort, represented by a partial palisade erected above the archaeological footprint of the original 1607 fort. The Jamestown Rediscovery project was launched in 1994. In 1996, the team of archaeologists led by William Kelso announced the finding of the original fort location even though for years it was thought to have been eroded by the shifting tides of the James River. Kelso recalled asking a park ranger where the fort site was. The ranger pointed to a lone cypress tree growing way offshore and said, "It's out there—and lost for good." Kelso was disappointed but kept looking, and he found the outline of the fort with only one corner lost to the James.

The importance of finding the fort is not just to know exactly where it was although that is exciting. The hundreds of thousands of artifacts uncovered from the site of James Fort have revealed a wealth of knowledge about the earliest years of the settlement and the men who struggled to make Jamestown survive. After finding the fort, archaeologists knew exactly where to dig to get the earliest archaeological records of the settlement. Much of what happened then happened inside those walls. Until the fort was found, the earliest history of Jamestown depended largely on the diaries or writings of a few men, including John Smith, and, while that written record is interesting, it is not complete. Some of the writings do not agree, so which is true? Archaeology may finally be able to give some answers.

The key to finding the fort, by the way, was knowing how to read dirt. Wood rots and colors the earth, and you can learn to distinguish what were once the sites of fence posts, postholes, and palisade walls. Though earlier excavations, including those under the direction of J.C. Harrington, had uncovered some features of James Fort, the methods for excavating seventeenth-century sites were still evolving, so the archaeologists were unable to adequately identify what had been found. Kelso and the

Chimney excavation.

Jamestown Rediscovery archaeologists benefited from both the data of previous excavations and developments in historical archaeology as a science. The archaeological excavations since then have

produced the latest from our earliest days. Jamestown is not silent. It talks to us through relics that demonstrate how we lived and died four hundred years ago.

If you stand in the church tower, you are standing about where the wall ran from the north corner (to your right) to the east corner by the riverbank. Keep in mind that the fort is more or less a triangle. The longest wall, roughly 140 yards, was along the river, facing south. The other two walls, which met at the north corner, were each about 100 yards long, the length of a football field without the end zones. The west point is the bit that is underwater. The fort enclosed just over an acre, about a third smaller than some earlier estimates based on written descriptions.

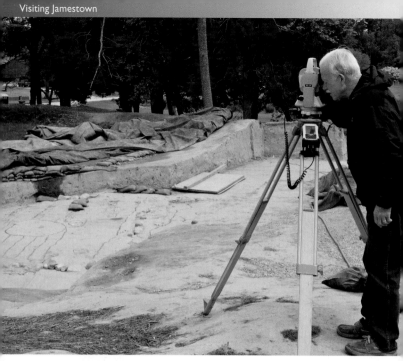

Archaeologist Bill Kelso using electronic distance-measuring device.

The walls were palisades made of split logs or saplings, chopped down and set straight up in the earth, and probably held together with wooden planks. Examples of split-log palisades have been reconstructed above the original remains so you can see what it would have looked like. From the outside, cannons and armed men would have been visible at the bulwarks, or corner positions. There were cannons at the three corners, so two of the three sets of guns were generally aimed at the river. Remember, the expected attackers were the Spanish, not the Virginia Indians, and they would sail in, not walk.

To make the dig more challenging, the site of James Fort is also the site of a Confederate fort built two and a half centuries later. To help you make sense of four hundred years' worth of layers of earth, interpreters are on hand to explain the current project, point out archaeological features, and answer questions.

Recovery of distiller's boiler jar.

Hunt Monument, Dale House, and Graveyard

After crossing through James Fort, follow the path to the Voorhees Archaearium. On the way, you'll encounter a monument to the Reverend Robert Hunt of the Church of England, one of the original settlers and the first Anglican minister in North America. While the *Susan Constant*, the *Discovery*, and the *Godspeed* waited for decent weather for six weeks at anchorage in the Thames, Hunt's determination, despite his own violent seasickness, helped keep the settlers committed. The first Communion at Jamestown's first church is depicted in the bronze bas-relief at Hunt's memorial.

Along the river not far from the Hunt shrine is the Dale House. Originally built in 1912 as the island's first visitor center, it's now a café where you can find food and drink and a seat under cover with a beautiful view of the James River.

The large wooden cross near the Voorhees Archaearium is in front of one of the places where the settlers buried their dead, and there were a lot of them. Between 1607 and 1625, about 5,000 people arrived in Jamestown, and others were born here after the first women arrived in 1608, but the census of 1625 found only 1,218 people alive. Think about that for a moment. Not good odds.

Archaearium

The Nathalie P. and Alan M. Voorhees Archaearium [ark-ee-AIR-ee-um] is an innovative approach to showcasing the findings of the Jamestown Rediscovery project. Built above the remains of

Jamestown's last statehouse, the Voorhees Archaearium allows you to see portions of the excavated ruins through sections of glass flooring. The 7,500-square-foot space tells the story of Jamestown through state-of-the-art exhibits, including virtual reality technology. Galleries highlight the settlers' voyage from England, the construction of James Fort, and the people of Jamestown.

Curators sifted through more than a million artifacts excavated at Jamestown to choose those that best articulated how archaeologists learned about life in the settlement. In each gallery, artifacts are placed in the context of their discovery. For example, an early James-town well uncovered in 2003 has been meticulously re-created with dozens of objects, including an almost full suit of armor, suspended within it just as they were discovered by archaeologists.

There are also videos showing the remains of buildings, wells, and artifacts as they were unearthed. You'll learn how archaeologists found the fort and see displays of arms and armor, medical instruments, amusements, and food remains. Interactive digital viewing stations put the seventeenth-century fort back on the landscape.

Here is also where dead men's tales are told. You can investigate, for example, the four-hundred-year-old mystery of who shot JR. No, not the villain from the TV show *Dallas*. "JR" in this case is short for Jamestown Rediscovery 102C, the first burial unearthed inside the fort. A resin cast of the skeleton is on display.

This JR seems to have been a gentleman. His bones show that he was not accustomed to hard labor, and the fact that he was buried in a coffin also indicates high status. A bullet in his lower right leg appears to have smashed the bone and probably severed an artery, killing him.

So, who fired the shot? Ballistic tests and X-rays determined that JR didn't shoot himself. The weapon was a European firearm, which clears the Indians. It may have been murder, possibly the result of political infighting, but it's more likely that it was an accident while he was hunting or participating in military exercises.

Pocahontas and John Smith

They were America's Romeo and Juliet; their story, Henry Adams wrote, was "the most romantic episode in the whole history of [the] country." Alas, there never was a love affair between John Smith and Pocahontas. In 1607, Pocahontas was about ten years old; John Smith was twenty-seven. She may have had a crush on him, but it was no more than that. It was John Rolfe, not John Smith, whom she married in 1614. Whatever the relationship between Smith and Pocahontas, it was not a romantic one, nor did Smith ever claim otherwise.

Yet the relationship was indeed a special one. Pocahontas came to the aid of the new colony a number of times, and, according to Smith's *Generall Historie of Virginia, New-England, and the Summer Isles,* she twice saved his life. The first time was in December 1607 when Smith led a trading party up the Chickahominy River. He was captured by Indians and taken before the great chief Powhatan. Then, just as Powhatan's warriors were about to "beate out his braines," Pocahontas threw herself between Smith and the warriors. At that point, Smith explained, Powhatan "was contented he should live to make him hatchets, and her bells."

Is Smith's story true?

Adams certainly didn't think so. He pointed out that Smith's earlier histories of Virginia make no mention of Pocahontas saving him; it was not until the 1624 *Generall Historie* that Smith published the story. By then, Adams argued, those who could have refuted it—such as Pocahontas herself—were dead. With no other English-speaking witnesses besides Pocahontas, it came down to Smith's word.

The rest of the *Generall Historie* didn't seem to do much to increase the value of that word. Smith told some remarkable—some would say incredible—tales. Seemingly least credible of all was that Pocahontas was just one of a series of foreign ladies who, unable to resist Smith's charms, came to his rescue. Before coming to Virginia, Smith had joined Austrian armies fighting against the Turks. He was captured and made a slave in Constantinople. There his luck improved: his mistress, "the beauteous Lady Tragabigzanda," took a liking to him, treated him well, and then sent him to her brother in Tartary, from where he escaped. He ultimately reached a Russian garrison where "the charitable Lady Callamata supplied my necessities."

All this about a man whose portraits are distinctly underwhelming. No wonder that some of Smith's contemporaries, and many historians, dismissed Smith as a braggart.

Then, in 1953, historian Laura Striker Polanyi carefully checked Smith's narrative of the wars against the Turks, and, to almost everyone's surprise, everything that could be checked turned out to be accurate. The case for Smith was further strengthened by ethnohistorians whose work showed that Smith's descriptions of Indian life and culture were realistic. Geographers, too, came to admire the accuracy of Smith's maps of the Chesapeake Bay and New England.

Why, then, didn't Smith write anything about the rescue until 1624? Maybe, his defenders have argued, he was embarrassed that he needed a child to save him. Or maybe Smith, whose life was full of hairbreadth escapes from death, simply didn't consider the story that important. He had no way of knowing that a few words in the *Generall Historie* were to become the basis of a nation's favorite love story.

Still, the story just doesn't make sense. Smith said he was spared "to make him

hatchets, and her bells." Powhatan had no shortage of hatchets or bells. Nor is there any reason to believe a powerful warrior and chief would be swayed by his daughter's plea.

This does not necessarily mean Smith made up the incident. Very possibly, it took place as Smith described it, but he misunderstood what was going on. According to Smith, the Indians fed him extravagantly and paraded him before the various tribes; right before they were to kill him, one Indian woman brought him water to wash his hands and another brought feathers to dry them. All this sounds like a carefully orchestrated ceremony. The "rescue" may also have been part of the ceremony.

Many historians have suggested that the rescue was part of a traditional ritual of death and rebirth that accompanied adoption into an Indian tribe. The archaeologist and historian Ivor Noël Hume argued that it was not a traditional ritual but a conscious effort on Powhatan's part to try to turn Smith into an ally. To have executed Smith, Noël Hume noted, would have been to bring down on Powhatan the wrath of the English, and Smith had made clear there were plenty more Englishmen across the water. Better to stage a ceremony that might leave Smith both intimidated and grateful—which was just the effect it had.

Pocahontas Saving Capt. John Smith (detail) from Theodore de Bry,
Grands Voyages, Frankfurt, Germany, 1626–1627.

STATUES

Jamestown Island is where John Smith and Pocahontas met, and there are statues of both here. We hate to do this to you, but they were not lovers. When Smith arrived at Jamestown, he would have been about twenty-seven, and she would have been about ten or eleven. Even in the early 1600s, that sort of liaison would have been frowned upon.

Neither of them is buried here. Smith suffered a gunpowder burn and returned to England in October 1609. He never returned to Virginia. When he died in 1631, he was buried in London.

Pocahontas was kidnapped by the English, converted to Christianity, baptized, and married in 1614 to John Rolfe, the settler who developed a commercial strain of Virginia tobacco. Known as Rebecca, Pocahontas sailed to England and was popular at court in London. In 1617, as she was beginning her journey home, she became very ill. She died in Gravesend, England, where she is buried.

Smith's statue on a column looking over the James was unveiled in 1909. Pocahontas's statue was also on a column when it was erected in 1922, but it had to be relocated when roads on Jamestown Island were reconfigured in the 1950s, so the brass likeness is now at eye level and, for that reason, friendlier.

You are walking where they walked.

NEW TOWNE

The 1907 Tercentenary Monument stands between the original settlement, where the fort was, and New Towne (to your left, if you're facing the river).

As the settlement expanded beyond the fort, rows of houses and warehouses were built in New Towne along two parallel roads: "Fronte Street" along the river and "Backstreete" further inland. By the middle of the seventeenth century, though probably there were still no more than a few hundred inhabitants, Jamestown was a bustling port, a manufacturing center, and a seat of government.

The bricks at New Towne are reproductions, not the foundations of seventeenth-century buildings. The actual foundations have been reburied to protect them from erosion. Still, you can stand right on top of them, and you can sense the excitement archaeologists must have felt as they tried to figure out what each site once was.

At one, for example, lots of pipe stems and wine bottle fragments were the keys to figuring out where a tavern stood. The General Assembly may have met on the same site, since it sometimes rented large public spaces for its meetings. At another New Towne site, lime from oyster shells, bog ore from the nearby swamp, and charcoal from burned trees were the clues that suggested iron smelting. Pieces of a copper kettle and cistern hinted that another site was where Jamestown brewed its ale. A 1772 French coin may

have been dropped by a French soldier bivouacked at Jamestown on his way to the 1781 siege of Yorktown.

At the sites of people's homes, pipes, iron handles and hinges, brass buckles, andirons, tin plates, wine bottles, thimbles, and musket barrels gave a sense of everyday life. At the May-Hartwell site, archaeologists glimpsed how the wealthier lived in Jamestown. Several glass bottles were stamped HH. They probably belonged to Henry Hartwell, clerk of the General Assembly, who must have had the seals applied to European wine bottles before having them shipped to Virginia. Elaborate ironwork found at the site of seventeenth-century row houses indicated that they must have once been quite elegant.

To the east end of the newer section are the ruins of the Ambler mansion. Richard Ambler moved to Virginia in 1716, by which time Jamestown had already lost its central role in Virginia. The Ambler family first built on the site about 1750. The house burned during the Revolutionary War, the Civil War, and finally in 1895.

Much of Jamestown was torched in 1676 by Nathaniel Bacon and his followers. They were angry about what they believed was an inadequate response to Indian raids on their frontier farms. Jamestown struggled on as the capital for another twenty-two years, but, when the statehouse burned again, the capital was moved to Williamsburg, and Jamestown became a James River plantation owned by the Ambler and Travis families. Until the APVA effort, it was, more or less, forgotten.

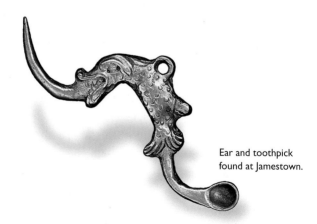

Ear and toothpick found at Jamestown.

ISLAND DRIVE

When you finish touring the area around the fort and town site, drive the three- or five-mile, one-lane Jamestown Island Drive. The short route goes only to the middle of the island; the other, all the way around. There are stops along the way with signs that tell you more about the island. In summertime, it takes almost no imagination to see the dark clouds of mosquitoes rising at sunset to make the settlers miserable. And diseased. And, yet, the island is lovely. The view of and across the river can be stunning. For those first few days, during spring in Virginia, it must have been a delight. You can imagine men accustomed to the fog, drizzle, and chill of London thinking they might have discovered a paradise. They would soon enough know that they had not.

They were not, of course, the only people in the region. Indians of the Powhatan chiefdom lived nearby, though none on Jamestown Island, perhaps because they had better sense than to make a swamp,

however defensible or beautiful, their home. The closest peoples were the Paspaheghs and the Chickahominys to the west.

On the Island Drive, you can see mulberry trees, another reminder of Jamestown's many failed enterprises. Mulberry trees were imported from Europe because they hosted silkworms, whose cocoons could be spun into cloth. The settlers came not for freedom but for the promise of fortune. Most of the settlers never found their fortune. Some people hunted for gold here, reasoning that, if the Spanish had found gold and silver in South America, why shouldn't it be here as well? It was not, and at least two ships carried cargoes of worthless dirt flecked with mica back to England to be tested for gold when they could have carried timber.

Of course, it's easy to be critical when we already know there is no commercial gold in Virginia. The settlers did not know that. They wanted to exploit and profit from the natural resources of the New World, but they did not understand what those resources were.

GLASSHOUSE

Before leaving Historic Jamestowne, stop at the Glasshouse, which is back on the mainland just over the causeway; you passed it as you entered Historic Jamestowne. The remains of the 1608 glasshouse were unearthed during a 1948–1949 dig. The Jamestown colonists attempted to establish a glass factory in the fall of 1608. The enterprise folded within six months, and a second effort, in 1620, failed as well. In 1624, the project was abandoned. Still, the unassuming remains of the original stone furnaces are a sign of early American commerce and industry.

What did artisans at the glasshouse make? Your guess is as good as anyone else's, but we do know that ordinary windowpane was in demand in England at that time, and, if you are trying to sell something, the logical idea is to make what people want. All we know with certainty is that there was "a tryall of glass" shipped in 1608.

The reproduction glasshouse, a few steps away, features colonial glassblowing demonstrations that are fun to watch. Glassblowers start with a blob of orange, molten glass called a "gather" that they pull from the furnace (at a temperature of about two thousand degrees Fahrenheit) and then blow, mold, and shape into a variety of objects you would have found in seventeenth-century Jamestown homes. Wine bottles and decanters, drinking glasses, saltcellars, and other hand-shaped items made by the costumed tradespeople are for sale adjacent to the work area.

Archaeological discoveries are bringing new excitement and new meaning to Jamestown. People are learning that the first permanent English settlement in North America was Jamestown, not Plymouth. Pocahontas lived in Virginia, not Massachusetts. By the time the Pilgrims arrived, she had been dead for three years. Jamestown, however, was alive.

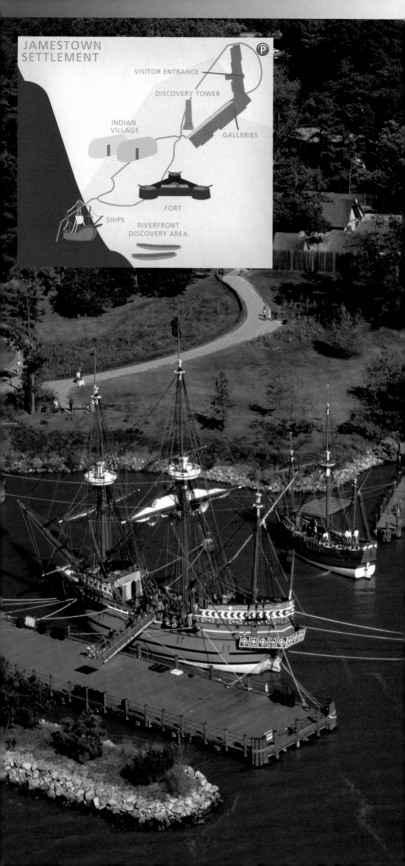

JAMESTOWN
SETTLEMENT

VISITOR ENTRANCE

DISCOVERY TOWER

INDIAN
VILLAGE

GALLERIES

FORT

SHIPS

RIVERFRONT
DISCOVERY AREA

WHAT TO SEE AT JAMESTOWN SETTLEMENT

www.historyisfun.org
1-888-593-4682 or 757-253-4838

Jamestown Settlement is not on Jamestown Island, but adjacent to it. While Historic Jamestowne, on the island across the causeway, is where the settlers actually settled, you have to imagine much of what was. At Jamestown Settlement, you don't have to imagine it; the world of the settlers and the Indians has been re-created for you. Outside, you can explore an Indian village and a settlers' fort and even board full-size replicas of the *Susan Constant*, the *Discovery*, and the *Godspeed*. The Settlement's indoor exhibits include buildings, dioramas, and artifacts that show how English, Indian, and African cultures converged in Virginia.

Jamestown Settlement helps you understand what you saw or will see at Historic Jamestowne. The two places are perfectly complementary.

GALLERIES

On your arrival at Jamestown Settlement, you'll enter a large building that houses visitor services, an education wing, a café, and the indoor galleries.

In the Robert V. Hatcher, Jr. Rotunda, a second-floor gallery shows special exhibits that change from time to time. A theater just off the rotunda shows the film *1607: A Nation Takes Root.* Both the film and the adjacent galleries offer an excellent overview of Jamestown's first two decades and the cultures that converged there. The film's opening scenes depict the natural beauty of 1607 Virginia, as Powhatan Indians observe English ships on the horizon. The film chronicles Jamestown's early years, shifting among Virginia, London, and Africa and concluding with the stories of some of those people "who struggled, persevered, and laid the foundation of a new country."

The main galleries, composed of a large, twisting gallery and an adjoining hall, house exhibits that examine events in Europe, Africa, and America that led to the founding of Jamestown. The galleries also chronicle the first century of the colony and describe the cultures of the Powhatan Indians, Europeans, and Africans who converged in seventeenth-century Virginia.

The hall, which you will enter first, has a time line and graphics of all kinds, but it is two-dimensional. Text and pictures, that's it. If you want just the basics—who did what when, rather a bare-bones presentation—it's here. If you're in a hurry and you want the quickest and easiest route, walk straight down the hall, but it's a shame. You'll miss truly impressive exhibits you cannot see anywhere else.

In the main gallery, which you can enter to your left as you walk down the hall, you can follow a path through the exhibits and get a more detailed idea of what went on before the settlers arrived and

for the century after they did. The museum is filled with rare artifacts. A blue onyx cameo brooch was supposedly given to Pocahontas in London. A Siegburg jar may have been presented to Pocahontas by King James and Queen Anne in 1617. A 1578 Bishops' Bible was the official Bible for the Church of England before the publication of the King James version in 1611; one like it was surely used in Jamestown. A silver-gilt steeple cup, dating from 1616, is much like those that were used in lotteries, one of the Virginia Company's methods for raising money. A pamphlet published by the Virginia Company in 1620 contains the first published description of the company's organization, a list of stockholders, and accounts of ships and cargoes sent to Virginia. A reproduction of Powhatan's mantle (the original is in Oxford, where in 1638 it was displayed as the "robe of the king of Virginia") is made from deer hides and decorated with beaded animal figures.

Many of the exhibits are interactive. You can, for example, touch deerskin, a bone fishhook, and freshwater pearls that represent Powhatan culture; an iron ax, copper bracelets, an iron fishhook, and bark cloth that represent African culture; and coins and a seal ring representing English culture. Interactive maps let you touch buttons to light sections detailing, for example, European exploration and the advance of English settlement.

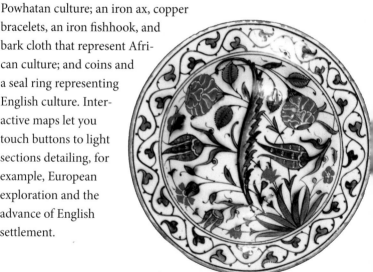

Turkish ceramic dish, 1585–1600.

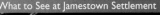

Before Jamestown

The first third or so of the gallery is devoted to the period before 1607. Much of what's here is based on what has been learned in the last ten to fifteen years, during which scholars have paid much more attention to the Indian and African cultures, as well as the European context for Jamestown's founding.

Until recently, the Jamestown story usually started with, "The Jamestown settlers arrived in 1607." That is true, but it gave you no reason or context for their arrival, nor any sense of what was here *before* they arrived. Global trade was already well under way, European countries were founding overseas colonies, some were finding riches in the Americas, and Great Britain wanted a piece of the action. The Spanish had explored the Chesapeake Bay as early as the 1520s. So, America did not start in 1607. Nor did Africa start when Europeans first took blacks as slaves. Still, at Jamestown, European, African, and American Indian cultures came together and stayed together, with eventual success, at least for the Europeans. For African Americans and Indians, the results were more often tragic, though their roles in shaping the new American culture were no less crucial for that.

The Atlantic World

In the past few decades, many historians have broadened their focus from Jamestown to the larger world of which it was a part.

"The history of Jamestown ... is better served when we view it in an Atlantic frame," wrote historian Karen Ordahl Kupperman. "The Atlantic perspective provides a more realistic context for English thinking about overseas ventures. It aims to understand the place of colonies as contemporaries did."

This Atlantic perspective extends north to Quebec, in what's now Canada, where, in 1608, just a year after the founding of Jamestown, the French established their first permanent settlement. This perspective encompasses the Lost Colony of Roanoke, which the English settled in the 1580s off the coast of what's now North Carolina and whose mysterious disappearance has been a source of intrigue and speculation ever since. A broader perspective also includes the Pilgrims, who landed in what's now Massachusetts in 1620 and who many Americans—wrongly—still think created the first permanent English colony.

Before the French or the British, there were the Spaniards, whose empire included large tracts of Central and South America and the Caribbean. The Spanish established the first permanent European settlement in North America as well, in the 1560s at St. Augustine in what's now Florida. The English were very much aware of the Spanish presence in America; in fact, Roanoke was originally founded as a base for attacking Spanish ships. The Spanish also set the precedent of plantations with African slave labor long before the first blacks arrived at Jamestown in 1619.

Some historians, like James Horn, have looked across the Atlantic to England noting that, until the final decades of the seventeenth century, the majority of Virginia's settlers were immigrants. "Men and women who moved to the Chesapeake," Horn wrote, "saw themselves, not as social outcasts exiled to a foreign land or as a chosen people on God's errand, but as participants in a vibrant and interconnected transatlantic world."

Indians, too, were looking at the Atlantic, on which they'd watched European ships sail for decades before 1607. Some Indians, like the chief the Spanish called Don Luis de Velasco, lived in Europe before returning to their people. To Europeans, these visitors often seemed a novelty act, but men like Don Luis were gathering information that later informed Indian strategies.

Historians have also broadened their perspective by drawing on other disciplines. Ethnohistorians, for example, have used the techniques of anthropology to better understand Indian culture, throwing new light on what Pocahontas may have actually intended when she threw herself between John Smith and the tomahawks of her father's warriors. Literary scholars have delved into the writings of Smith and others, placing them in the context of such contemporaries as William Shakespeare and increasing our understanding of them as both historical documents and literary works. Dendrochronologists, who study tree rings, have discovered that the Jamestown settlers arrived in the midst of a horrendous seven-year drought, which helps explain why the colony so nearly perished. Archaeologists have uncovered evidence of the original fort at Jamestown, long thought to have been washed into the James River.

"The result of such interdisciplinarity," Kupperman wrote, "is a far richer picture of the past."

Virginiae Item et Floridae Americae Provinciarum nova Descriptio (detail) by Henricus Hondius, 1606.

The gallery starts with what Virginia—the land, the animals, the landscape—was like before it was Virginia. About twenty to twenty-five years before the English would arrive, the Powhatan chiefdom was forming, consisting of more than thirty separate Indian peoples living in the region. Its great chief was Wahunsonacock, who came to be known as Powhatan. Other peoples, however, had lived in the area long before the Powhatans. An archaeological dig south of Richmond at Cactus Hill, about fifty miles south southwest of Jamestown, found artifacts carbon-dated to fifteen or sixteen thousand years ago. The exhibit includes a diorama of Powhatan culture, including a full-size house.

A section on Africa focuses on Angola, the original home of the slaves who were traded for supplies at Jamestown in 1619. At that time, the Portuguese, who were slave traders, were fighting a war with the Ndongans, a Bantu people in northern Angola. The Portuguese had taken thousands of prisoners, many of whom were sold into slavery. Some of the Ndongans were loaded on the *Sao João Bautista* at Luanda, Angola, to be sold at Vera Cruz, Mexico. In the Gulf of Mexico, a Dutch ship and an English ship attacked the *Sao João Bautista* and divided its cargo. The Dutch ship, the *White Lion,* brought some of the slaves to Jamestown. There is no record of what happened to the other Ndongans.

Ndongans lived in small villages and towns surrounded by palisades. Most practiced traditional African religions, but, by the seventeenth century, many had adopted elements of Christianity. Farmers harvested traditional African crops like sorghum, yams, and millet. They also grew tobacco and corn, which some would later grow as slaves in Virginia. The exhibit includes a life-size representation of a dwelling in Angola.

A section on England includes a street scene. The reconstructed houses are based on an actual block of row houses that once stood in London.

As Jamestown Settlement senior curator Thomas Davidson put it: "Life in Virginia prior to 1607, life in England prior to 1607, life in Angola prior to 1607."

CULTURAL INTERACTIONS

After the pre-1607 exhibits, you turn the corner and find the full-size bow of the *Susan Constant* sailing out of the wall. You can tour the bow, and there is also an interactive demonstration of stellar navigation.

Just in front of the bow are two exhibits. The closest is a room devoted to the Virginia Company of London, the group of merchants who financed the first settlement at Jamestown; without the Virginia Company, there would have been no Jamestown. The museum has graphics, paintings, and information on some of the more famous members of

the company, including the only known portrait executed during the lifetime of Thomas West, third Baron De La Warr. It was his timely arrival in 1610 with supplies and more settlers that saved Jamestown after the Starving Time. There's also a portrait of Henry Wriothesley, the third Earl of Southampton and a major investor in the company, though he never set foot in Virginia.

Another of the stockholders was the archbishop of Canterbury, head of the Church of England, the official religion of England and of Virginia, initially. He was an investor, and the church was a supporter. The Virginia Company mobilized the church to get out the word of the opportunity. The poet John Donne was commissioned to give sermons in support of colonization. For the church, Jamestown was a business venture mixed with a religious ideal—converting the Indians.

Incidentally, the military weapons and armor on display are authentic seventeenth-century artifacts, selected because they match archaeological discoveries at early seventeenth-century Virginia sites.

Near the bow of the *Susan Constant* is a theater with a short video on the voyage from London to Jamestown.

Next door to the theater is an Indian village model that is based on an archaeological dig of a nearby Paspahegh village. The model, depicting thirty-five buildings, is nearly twenty feet long. Exhibits explore the relationship between Virginia's colonists and the Indians, ranging from trade to conflict.

As you learn about how the English, Indian, and African cultures came together, you'll meet Pocahontas and learn about the tobacco economy. The gallery covers in detail the trade and conflict between the Indians and settlers as well as the lives of Africans in seventeenth-century Virginia and Africa. Both Africans and Indians, by the way, grew and smoked their own tobacco, though it was John Rolfe who developed a milder Virginia tobacco and tapped into a commercial market in Europe.

The museum devotes a great deal of space to the Powhatans, who did not disappear, even after 1646. That was the year the second Powhatan war ended. The Powhatan chief Opechancanough led that war and an earlier one in 1622. After 1646, the Indians had only limited political independence. The freedom of white settlers may have grown, but that of the Indians was shrinking.

Seventeenth-century Virginia Indian treaty badge.

LEGACIES OF JAMESTOWN

The last third of the exhibit is devoted to a mature colony and how it was owned, socially organized, and governed. An interactive map shows the spread of settlements. Tobacco wore out the land, forcing tobacco planters to move north and west.

Another exhibit covers the Church of England in Virginia and its influence on government. By law, settlers were required to go to church twice a day although there is some question of how strictly that law was enforced.

Near the end of the gallery are three full-size buildings: an American Indian's house, a slave's quarters, and a "middling" planter's home. The Indian house is a reconstruction of an actual late seventeenth-century Indian dwelling discovered by archaeologists at a site in Caroline County, Virginia, in 1964. You can see that Indians made extensive use of English tools: sections are fastened together with nails that would not be found in a traditional Indian house. Yet the house is still very different from those of the English.

The slave's quarters and the planter's home were built very similarly. A framework is supported by vertical posts sunk into earth, and the roof and sides of the buildings were made of hundreds of wooden boards nailed to the frame. Only a tiny minority of very wealthy Virginians could afford brick houses, or even brick fireplaces. The planter's home is a full-scale re-creation of one that belonged to Thomas Atkinson, who owned sixty-four acres of land and about whom much was learned during an archaeological dig in James City County.

Mixed in with the three buildings is an exhibit on how people lived in those days and on the clothing and textiles they used.

What are the legacies of Jamestown? Individualism, the rule of law, democracy, free enterprise, certainly, but also the exploitation of people and the environment and racial injustice. The settlers came not to change the world but to make England (and themselves) rich. Instead, they changed the world.

And now head outside, passing the Discovery Tower, originally intended as a companion piece to the Tercentenary Monument at Historic Jamestowne. You may notice the ferry on the river. It makes the fifteen-minute crossing, transporting people and vehicles, between Glass House Point at Jamestown and Scotland in Surry County.

The outside exhibits are in four areas, heading down to the James River and then back. The return walk is uphill but not steep. From some points along the path, you can see all four at once—a re-created Powhatan Indian village, replicas of the three ships that landed in 1607, a representation of the colonial fort, and a riverfront discovery area that explores waterway transportation and commercial activities. There is no one order to see the outdoor exhibits, but there is a logical path.

Indian Village

As you follow the sidewalk, you come first to the Indian village. It is based on archaeological research at Paspahegh, the closest Powhatan community to Jamestown. Several of the English colonists also left written descriptions of the village, so this is as close to reality as you are likely to find.

Some may be surprised there are no tents. Tepees were used by the nomadic Plains Indians. Virginia Indians had permanent homes although they might move depending on the needs of the tribe or the time of year. For instance, in deer season, part of the Paspahegh moved to the hunting area around what is now Richmond. Around Jamestown, Indians lived in yehakins, made by bending saplings and covering the young trees with bark or reed mats. An indoor fire kept them warm. One family lived in each house. English settlers described the homes as

dry, warm, and smoky. There are places for sleep and for storage. You'll see yehakins in the village; take the time to go inside.

The Indians who lived in the area they called Tsenacommacah had varying customs—remember, there were more than thirty tribes who made up the Powhatan chiefdom—but they all farmed, hunted, fished, tanned hides, made what they needed, cared for their tools and their weapons, and worshipped their gods. Costumed interpreters will be doing one or more of those things, depending on the season, and you can try your hand at grinding corn or playing corncob darts. In the village, there is a circle of logs set upright in the ground with faces carved on them. Common among the Algonquian Indians of coastal Carolina, this type of circle also may have been used by the Powhatans of Virginia for ceremonial purposes, though that's not certain.

Don Luis and Opechancanough

By the time John Smith and company disembarked at Jamestown, the area's native peoples were all too familiar with Europeans, and at least one chief had been to Europe.

This future chief was just a teenager in 1561 when two Spanish ships entered the Chesapeake Bay (or, as the Spaniards called it, Bahia de Santa Maria). The Spanish had a tendency to kidnap natives, and so the boy soon found himself en route to Spain. There he received a Catholic education, was baptized Don Luis de Velasco, and was introduced to King Philip II.

Nine years later, Don Luis returned to Virginia along with eight Jesuit missionaries and a young novice, Alonso de Olmos. They sailed up what was later called the James River to College Creek, just a few miles downriver from what would become Jamestown. Then they trekked over land to various creeks, paddled down to the future York River, and built a mission, the first European settlement in the region.

Had the Jesuit mission taken hold, the Spaniards might have followed up with a fort, and the English might have had a much tougher time establishing Jamestown. As it turned out, though, the mission didn't last long. Don Luis quickly returned to his own people. A few months later, the Spaniards, by then almost out of food, sent a search party to bring him back. Indians, perhaps under Don Luis's command, killed the three searchers, then the other five priests. Only Alonso was spared. Spanish ships returned in 1571 and 1572, reclaiming the novice (who recounted the fate of the Jesuits) and avenging the priests by killing many Indians.

What happened to Don Luis? Here's where the story really gets good.

One theory, championed by historian Carl Bridenbaugh, is that Don Luis was none other than Opechancanough, the brother and successor of Powhatan (the father of Pocahontas). Opechancanough's experiences with the Spanish, Bridenbaugh believed, instilled in him a lifelong desire to rid his land of Europeans. This led him to kill the lost colonists who wandered north from Roanoke to the Chesapeake and then to plan and lead attacks on the English in 1622 and 1644. In both cases, Opechancanough used the same strategy as Don Luis: lull the Europeans into thinking he was on their side and then launch sudden and surprise attacks. The 1622 attack killed 347 whites across Virginia and might have wiped out Jamestown had an Indian working as a servant across the river not alerted the settlers.

By 1644, Opechancanough was more than a hundred years old and was, Robert Beverley wrote just over fifty years later, "now grown so decrepit, that he was not able to walk alone; but was carried about by his Men, where-ever he had a Mind to move." Still, he managed to organize an attack that killed more than four hundred whites that year. Two years later, he was captured and shot in the back.

As evidence that Don Luis and Opechancanough were one and the same, Bridenbaugh pointed to rumors circulating among the British settlers that some Indian rulers had origins elsewhere and that Opechancanough displayed an understanding of astronomy that he could have gained in Spain. Beverley noted that the Powhatans considered Opechancanough "a Prince of a Foreign Nation."

Other historians accused Bridenbaugh of being ethnocentric. "Astronomical knowledge of that basic sort," wrote Helen Rountree, "is easily arrived at after only a

few years of casual observation, and anthropologists have found that most peoples in the world have at least that much knowledge." Moreover, Rountree argued, Don Luis's family ruled an area downriver from Powhatan's (and later Opechancanough's). Also, Opechancanough showed himself to be non-Europeanized when he, crucially, failed to follow up his 1622 and 1644 attacks.

Most historians have doubts about whether Don Luis and Opechancanough were one and the same, but few doubt that Opechancanough was a formidable chief. Wrote Bridenbaugh: "We may consider not only whether an elder brother, Opechancanough, did not far surpass [Powhatan] in talents and capacity for leadership but also if Opechancanough does not deserve to rank high among the most famous American Indians—with Massasoit, King Philip, Pontiac, Logan, Joseph Brant, Sitting Bull, Crazy Horse, and Geronimo."

Indian War Dance (detail) by
Baroness Hyde de Neuville, 1821.

SHIPS

As you leave the village, head for the pier where full-size re-creations of the *Susan Constant*, the *Godspeed*, and the *Discovery* are moored. Those three ships brought the original settlers in 1607. You may already have seen a picture of them on the Virginia quarter minted by the United States and issued in 2000.

The original *Susan Constant* was involved in a maritime accident on the River Thames in 1606, and the case wound up in court. As a result, we have from the court record some information on the original ship, a 120-ton merchantman. As good (or bad, from the perspective of historians) fortune would have it, neither the *Godspeed* nor the *Discovery* was ever involved in a court case so we know less about them. However, the ships were ordinary merchant vessels in commercial use, and we have a pretty clear idea of how much they could carry, based on their historically documented tonnage. The *Godspeed* was a 40-ton vessel; the *Discovery* a 20-ton vessel. As more is learned in research about tonnage and other factors, the sizes of the replicas change. The current replica of the *Godspeed*, which was commissioned in 2006, has an overall length of 88 feet, a mainmast of 72 feet, and a width (beam) of 17 feet.

No matter how you measure them, they are tiny, and you won't have to stand on the pier long before thinking, "People crossed the ocean in *that*?" The voyage was dangerous as well as cramped. Navigation was limited and there was no such thing as weather forecasting, so, if a hurricane or northeaster developed, too bad for you. There was no such thing as refrigeration either, or tin cans or plastic wrap or foil, so, by the end of the voyage, you would be faced with mold or maggots in your food. Remarkably, on the voyage in 1607, only one person died: Edward Brookes succumbed to heatstroke in the Caribbean.

The three ships went the long way round, south from the English coast to the Canary Islands; then to the Caribbean, stopping for fresh food and water and some time ashore; then north up the coast to the Chesapeake Bay. It was the standard route to America, taking advantage of prevailing winds. The three ships sailed from England December 20, 1606, spent six weeks anchored off the English coast waiting for good weather to sail, spent nineteen days in March and early April in the West Indies, and made the Chesapeake Bay April 26, 1607.

Why did they go? It is too easy to forget that settlers, even the poorest, had some chance, however small, at success. At least in Virginia there was some chance they might someday own their own land. Given the choice, it's unlikely many of the settlers would have returned to England, where they had no chance. Some chance beats no chance, and these three small sailing ships were headed toward some chance.

Christopher Newport was in command of the *Susan Constant* and the fleet. Bartholomew Gosnold captained the *Godspeed;* John Ratcliffe the *Discovery*. After arriving at Jamestown on May 13, sailors helped settlers build a three-sided fort, which was completed by June 16. Six days later, Newport headed the *Susan Constant* and the *Godspeed* back to London. The *Discovery* stayed in Virginia and was used by John Smith and others to explore the area. Gosnold stayed with the settlers, clearly intending to help lead them, but, two months after Newport sailed, Gosnold died and was buried with military honors. Ratcliffe also stayed and was captured and killed by Indians in the fall of 1609.

Depending on maintenance schedules and trips to various ports, one or more of the replica ships are open, and you can walk around above and belowdecks. You don't know how small the ships really are until you go below. Imagine that many people—seventy or so on the *Susan Constant* alone—crammed into that little space for that length of time and not bathing for most of the time. The space between decks would have reeked. Ask the historical interpreters about the 1607 voyage and shipboard life.

RIVERFRONT

When you leave the pier, head back toward the galleries, but take the sidewalk that leads toward the fort not the Powhatan village. You'll come to the riverfront discovery area, a few structures and some exhibits in front of the fort where you might learn how to make a map or scrape out a tree trunk to make a canoe.

The rivers around the Chesapeake Bay were the Interstate Highway System of that time. The Indians used canoes, made by hollowing out cedar logs, some of them fifty feet long. The settlers brought a disassembled shallop, a boat that could be rowed or sailed in less water than the *Discovery*, rather like a flat-bottomed barge. It was used for transportation, expeditions, and trade with the Indians. River travel was essential to Jamestown's survival. So was river food. All three cultures—Indian, European, and African—knew how to fish and shared techniques.

FORT

Just beyond the discovery area is a re-creation of the Jamestown fort, based on a 1610 description by settler William Strachey. It is about a mile away from the site of the original on Jamestown Island. The Virginia Company required the settlers to build three public buildings before they built anything else—a church, a storehouse, and a guardhouse. These settlers were not seeking religious freedom, as would the Pilgrims thirteen years later at Plymouth, but they were faithful Church of England worshippers. They had to have the storehouse both to protect their own supplies and to keep those items they planned to send back to England. The guardhouse was the headquarters of those who guarded the fort, and it also served as an arsenal.

Costumed interpreters can help you understand what is happening at the fort, and you can walk in, wander about, and touch much of what you see. What's happening depends on the time of year and the schedule. You may see some teenaged boys trying on helmets and body armor, posing proudly for a smiling teenage girl with a digital camera. Some of the original settlers would not have been much older when they put on the armor and prepared to fight for their survival.

From the fort, it's a quick walk back to the main building.

Jamestown Settlement provides an entertaining view of history. But, this is history, not Hollywood; fact, not fantasy. A lot of people died at Jamestown—Indians, Europeans, Africans—but, in the end, from this place, the United States emerged.

Visiting
Williamsburg

Dr. W. A. R. Goodwin, President Franklin D. Roosevelt, Eleanor Roosevelt, and navy captain Wilson Brown at the gates of Bruton Parish Church, 1936 (above). Duke of Gloucester Street, ca. 1928 (opposite).

THE RESTORATION

*I*n 1926, the restoration of Virginia's colonial capital started with the purchase of a single eighteenth-century house. Nine years later, an architectural magazine gave a synopsis of what had been done:

> Some 440 buildings of late construction have been torn down and 18 moved outside the Colonial area; 66 Colonial buildings have been repaired or restored; 84 have been reproduced upon Colonial foundations. Federal Highway 60 has been diverted to a by-pass road, and streets, open spaces and gardens have resumed their Colonial appearance, with lamp-posts, fences, brick walks, street surfaces and plantings derived from authentic records.

Eleven years later, Kenneth Chorley, the second president of Colonial Williamsburg, Inc., spoke of the need, amid the ongoing physical restoration projects, to think in terms of education and interpretation. The dual tasks of restoration and education continue to this day.

How did the restoration of Williamsburg start? Who thought of it, who financed it, and what did they want to accomplish?

Much of the credit goes to Dr. W. A. R. (William Archer Rutherfoord) Goodwin, the Episcopal rector of Bruton Parish Church, who moved from Petersburg to Williamsburg in 1903 and began the restoration of the church in 1905. Being able to restore the church to its eighteenth-century condition was part of the agreement to persuade

Duke of Gloucester Street, ca. 1890.

him to move. The restoration was completed in 1907, in time for the three hundredth anniversary of the settlement of Jamestown.

Goodwin's goal was to restore not only the church but the entire town. Reasoning that it was the automobile, more than any other device, that was destroying the colonial character of the town, he first asked Henry Ford, through his son, Edsel, for the money. If Goodwin was brilliant at colonial history and concepts of restoration, he was sometimes a little short on tact, telling Edsel Ford, "You and your father are at present the chief contributors to the destruction of this city." Henry Ford said he was "unable to interest himself in the matter mentioned."

Next Goodwin persuaded local people, including the Colonial Dames of America, to buy the George Wythe House as Bruton Parish's rectory, and he supervised its restoration. In 1924, Goodwin spoke in New York to the Phi Beta Kappa Society, whose origins date back to 1776 at the College of William and Mary, and he met John D. Rockefeller Jr., whom he eventually persuaded to visit Williamsburg. Two years later, Rockefeller was at William and Mary for the dedication of Phi Beta Kappa Memorial Hall. He toured the restored George Wythe House and, by himself, wandered around Williamsburg, then a sleepy backwater of gas stations and mechanic shops and factories left over from World War I. But, if you knew what you

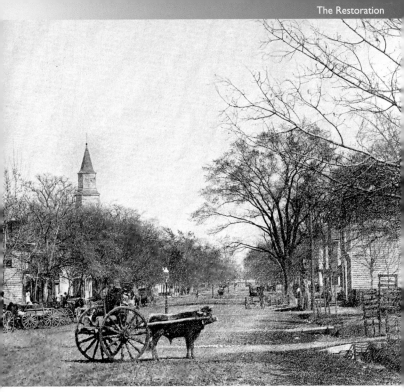

were looking at, Goodwin said, "Williamsburg is the one remaining Colonial village which any man could buy."

So Rockefeller did.

Rockefeller said that the opportunity to restore a whole town was something he could not resist, and that was what Goodwin offered—not a building, not a street, not a complex, but a whole town. All of it.

In December 1926, the Ludwell-Paradise House came on the market for eight thousand dollars. Goodwin sent a letter on December 4 to Rockefeller to suggest that he buy it. Three days later, Rockefeller answered by telegram: "Authorize purchase of antique referred to in your long letter of December fourth at eight." The telegram was signed "Davids father," preserving Rockefeller's anonymity and thus holding down prices.

Dr. W.A.R Goodwin, engineer Robert Trimble, John D. Rockefeller Jr., and landscape architect Arthur Shurcliff.

Ludwell-Paradise was the first property bought, but the first property restored was the Bracken Tenement. Work started June 1, 1928. The Raleigh Tavern opened as the first exhibition building in September 1932. By 1934, when the first phase of the reconstruction was finished, Williamsburg was well on its way to being one of the most elegant towns in America. Franklin Roosevelt, serving his first term, came to Williamsburg to praise what had been done: "What a thrill it has been . . . to have the honor of formally opening the reconstructed Duke of Gloucester Street . . . and see the transformation which has taken place, to see the Capitol, the Governor's Palace, the Raleigh Tavern born again; to see sixty-one colonial buildings restored, ninety-four colonial buildings rebuilt; the magnificent gardens of colonial days reconstructed—in short to see how thorough the renaissance of these physical landmarks,

Prentis Store, pre- and post-restoration (above). The Magazine when used as a stable, 1877–1890 (below).

Dr. W.A.R. Goodwin and John D. Rockefeller Jr., 1928.

the atmosphere of a whole glorious chapter in our history, has been recaptured."

Roosevelt dedicated Duke of Gloucester Street as "the most historic avenue in America."

William Archer Rutherfoord Goodwin died in September 1939, and John D. Rockefeller Jr. died in May 1960. One had the early inspiration and vision but not the money; the other had the money and shared the vision. Together they restored Virginia's colonial and Revolutionary capital.

The Revolutionary City

It was here in Williamsburg that American independence—and democracy—took root. The events that played out here before and during the Revolution are replayed again on the streets of Colonial Williamsburg's Historic Area in an innovative and acclaimed street theater program, Revolutionary City.

The program takes place every day at the east end of the Historic Area, near the Capitol. Some of the characters you'll meet, such as Patrick Henry, Benedict Arnold, and George and Martha Washington, are well-known. Others, such as Barbry Hoy, the wife of a carpenter-turned-soldier, and Gowan Pamphlet, an African-American preacher, do not appear in most traditional histories. All these people and many others—men and women, patriots and Tories, free and enslaved—played their roles in the Revolution.

Similarly, the scenes you'll see in Revolutionary City mix events both grand and everyday. You may see, for example, the royal governor, Lord Dunmore, dissolving the House of Burgesses or Virginia's representatives deciding on independence or Washington's troops marching to Yorktown. But you may also see Ariana Randolph, a loyalist mother, warning her daughter Susannah that her father's loyalty to the king may mean the family will have to leave for England. Or Barbry Hoy, whose husband has been captured by the British, desperately seeking work. Or enslaved people gathering to consider whether to trust Dunmore's offer of freedom to those who will take up arms against their rebel masters.

The program takes place over three days. The first day covers events that led to the collapse of royal government between 1774 and 1776. Day two focuses on the lives of citizens at war from 1776 to 1781. Day three lets you learn more about some "nation builders." You don't have to see "Collapse of the Royal Government," "Citizens at War," and "Nation Builders" in sequence. You can choose any combination of scenes to weave together your own experience.

"In the Capitol, taverns, and coffeehouse, in the newspapers, and on the streets," explained James Horn, Colonial Williamsburg's vice president of Research and Historical Interpretation, "ordinary men and women debated what the American Revolution meant for them. By dramatizing colonial Americans' personal struggles for freedom in the Revolutionary City program, we invite all our guests to participate in the Revolution and be part of the story."

Indeed, during this interactive program, you don't just learn about the Revolution, you join it. You may very well be asked, as were the citizens of Williamsburg in 1776, "How say ye?" Would you have agreed that an outspoken loyalist should be tarred and feathered? Would you have stood up to Benedict Arnold when his troops occupied Williamsburg? As an enslaved lady's maid, would you have run to the British army?

Revolutionary City was designed not only to make you think about what it meant to live before and during the Revolution, when subjects of a monarchy found the courage to turn themselves into citizens of an independent republic. It also makes you consider what it means to be a twenty-first-century citizen, a participant in the ongoing experiment of democracy.

"Dissent is raging once again in these eighteenth-century streets," wrote *USA Today* about the program. "The costumed characters might be out of the Colonial era, but many of the themes—whether or not to support a war, for instance—have contemporary resonance."

WHAT TO SEE IN COLONIAL WILLIAMSBURG'S HISTORIC AREA

www.history.org

1-800-HISTORY or 757-229-1000

*W*alking down Duke of Gloucester Street, you may run into Alexander Hoy, a poor man who enlisted in the army and was captured at Charleston; you may find yourself among slaves debating whether to seek freedom by joining the British; you may join George Washington preparing to march his troops toward Yorktown; or you may jeer Benedict Arnold, the one-time Revolutionary and now British general whose troops occupy Williamsburg. This is the Revolutionary City, where you are caught up in the world-changing events that occurred here as America sought its independence.

The backdrop is Colonial Williamsburg's 301-acre Historic Area. Once you're here, you're in eighteenth-century America. Here, people are debating the Revolutionary ideas that continue to shape our nation. They are also living in the homes, cooking the food, working at the trades, and dressing in the clothes of the eighteenth century. Here are eighty-eight original eighteenth-century buildings, restored to look as they did then. Here, too, are many reconstructed buildings, often rebuilt on their original foundations. The buildings

in the Historic Area range from government buildings like the Capitol to colonial homes like those of Peyton Randolph and George Wythe, from the grandeur of the Governor's Palace to the grittiness of a blacksmith's shop.

Not only can you see what an eighteenth-century town looked like, but you can also talk to its people. On the streets and in the buildings of the Historic Area, you'll meet tradespeople, shopkeepers, slaves, maybe even Patrick Henry or Thomas Jefferson. And people weren't an eighteenth-century town's only inhabitants. Throughout the Historic Area, you'll also see sheep and oxen and cattle and horses (many pulling elegant carriages). Many of these are rare breeds preserved by Colonial Williamsburg.

Some of these buildings are lived in by twenty-first-century families, and those aren't open to the public. Yet, more than twenty-five are open, if you buy a ticket, providing an inside look at colonial

life. Ticket holders also can visit tradespeople working as they did in the eighteenth century. You can, for example, watch silversmiths hammer silver ingots into beautiful tableware or blacksmiths forge tools that are used throughout the Historic Area. Almost all the gardens in the Historic Area are open to the public, even those next to houses that are not. To wander through them is one of the area's many pleasures.

Colonial Williamsburg's extraordinary collections, ranging from furniture to folk art, can be seen at its art museums, the DeWitt Wallace Decorative Arts Museum and the Abby Aldrich Rockefeller Folk Art Museum.

After dark, there's still plenty to do in the Historic Area. You can listen to a balladeer at one of the taverns, follow a lantern-led tour to hear ghost stories and legends of the period, or watch an eighteenth-century play.

The heart of the Historic Area is Duke of Gloucester Street. "The most historic avenue in America" (as Franklin Roosevelt described

it) runs from the Capitol on the east end to the Wren Building at the College of William and Mary on the west, not quite a mile long and ninety-nine feet wide. It was the main street in the Revolutionary period. During the day, there is normally no motor vehicle traffic on Duke of Gloucester Street, except for designated cross streets, so watch yourself at intersections, but stroll down the middle of the street if you feel like it. However, you should keep in mind that there are horse-drawn carriage rides along Duke of Gloucester Street, so it would be to your advantage to be aware of where you are stepping.

At the west end of Duke of Gloucester Street, near the College of William and Mary, is Merchants Square, done in eighteenth-century architectural style but with modern stores and restaurants. This retail area extends one block on either side of Duke of Gloucester to Prince George and Francis Streets. There are no restrictions on traffic on

Prince George, Francis, and Boundary Streets, so be warned: you are back in the twenty-first century, and the cars and trucks are real.

The most comprehensive handbook on what to see in the Historic Area is *The Official Guide to Colonial Williamsburg*. For the day's schedule, programs, exhibitions, and events, "This Week" is essential. Pick one up with your ticket. Some programs require reservations as well as tickets.

VISITOR CENTER

Before heading into the Historic Area, it's worth a stop at the Visitor Center. Sure, you can pick up tickets other places as well, but here you can figure out all your options; make dining, program, and tour reservations; and also watch *Williamsburg—The Story of a Patriot*. This is not your usual orientation film. It's a Hollywood production whose director, writers, cast, and crew include several Academy Award winners. The film has been showing continuously since 1957, and its digital restoration set new standards. The restored movie premiered in 2004.

The Visitor Center also offers free parking.

From the Visitor Center, ticket holders can hop a bus to various points around the Historic Area. Buses shuttle between the Visitor Center and the Gateway Building, near the Governor's Palace. They also circle the Historic Area, with stops near the Capitol, Wetherburn's Tavern, the Magazine and Guardhouse, the Williamsburg Lodge, the Public Hospital, and Merchants Square.

Or you can walk across a bridge to the past. The bridge links the twenty-first to the eighteenth century. Bronze plaques in the deck of the bridge illustrate how life has changed since the American Revolution. On your return trip, plaques feature individuals and their contributions to the growth of our democracy.

Across the bridge, you're in the eighteenth century. A quarter-mile path leads past Great Hopes Plantation to the Gateway Building, where you can get an orientation walk and another chance to check on the day's openings and programs.

YOU HAVE RETURNED TO THE 21ST CENTURY

DEMOCRACY
A WORK IN PROGRESS

WALK BACK
IN TIME

YOU ARE LEAVING THE 21ST CENTURY

Stolen Powder

A day after the first fighting of the American Revolution broke out at Lexington and Concord in Massachusetts, a remarkably similar incident took place in Williamsburg. The trouble started, in both cases, when the British attempted to seize stockpiles of arms. In Massachusetts, Paul Revere sounded the warning, and, on April 19, 1775, the minutemen forced the British to retreat to Boston. In Virginia, the story played out differently.

For a week or so, Williamsburg's patriots had heard rumors that Lord Dunmore, Virginia's royal governor, was planning to steal their muskets and powder. Volunteers took turns guarding the magazine, the octagonal brick armory. Late in the night of April 21, bored after nothing happened, the volunteers headed home to bed. Then, a few hours after midnight, a small party of British seamen from the HMS *Magdalen* crept into the town, loaded about fifteen or twenty half kegs of powder onto a horse-drawn wagon, and headed out of town. Someone, it's not clear who, spotted or heard them, and an angry mob gathered at Market Square, next to the magazine. The Brits escaped, but there was talk of storming the Governor's Palace.

A delegation that included Peyton Randolph, Speaker of the House of Burgesses; John Dixon, mayor of Williamsburg; and Robert Carter Nicholas, treasurer of the colony, confronted Dunmore. The governor explained that he'd taken the powder only to protect the colonists against a rumored slave uprising. The delegation accepted this explanation and managed to disperse the mob.

Outside Williamsburg, patriots were not so easily mollified. In Hanover County, Patrick Henry led about 150 volunteers to within a few miles of Williamsburg before more moderate leaders convinced him to accept a bill of exchange for the value of the powder.

How to explain the parallel yet diverging events in Massachusetts and Virginia? For many patriots then and historians since, the parallel was no mere coincidence. They suspected British general Thomas Gage in Massachusetts and Dunmore in Virginia had both been carrying out orders from their superiors. Indeed, the colonists later learned that, early in 1775, all royal governors had received instructions to "take the most effectual measures for arresting, detaining, and securing any Gunpowder, or any sort of Arms or Ammunition."

Yet, those orders referred only to newly imported arms and gunpowder. They included no timetable, nor is there any evidence that Dunmore and Gage coordinated their raids. More likely, Dunmore was reacting to specific threats that had arisen in Virginia. In March, the Virginia Convention had met in St. John's Church in Richmond and urged colonists to take "a posture of Defense." It was there that Patrick Henry had given his famous—and to Dunmore undeniably worrisome—"give me liberty or give me death" speech. The Convention had also decided to send representatives to the Continental Congress in Philadelphia.

A May 1 letter from Dunmore to Lord Dartmouth, the British secretary of state, seems to confirm that the governor decided on his own to seize the powder. "The series of dangerous measures pursued by the People of this Colony against Government," he wrote, "which they have now entirely overturned, & particularly their having come to a Resolution of raising a Body of armed Men in all the Counties, made me think it prudent to remove some Gunpowder which was in a Magazine in this place."

In the same letter, Dunmore pretty much admitted that the alleged slave uprising was nothing but an excuse to calm down the colonists. "I thought proper," he explained to Dartmouth, "to sooth them and answered verbally to the effect that I had removed the Powder . . . lest the Negroes might have seized upon it." Dunmore clearly wasn't worried about black people seizing the ammunition; it was the white people of Virginia who, he rightly perceived, might use that ammunition against him.

As for the comparatively moderate response of Virginia's patriots, keep in mind that, at least initially, no one in Williamsburg knew about events in Lexington and Concord. That news, which would increase the anger of patriots, didn't reach Williamsburg until a week later. Moreover, patriot leaders like Randolph felt a united front

at the Continental Congress would have more impact on British policy than a riot in Williamsburg. And, though Dunmore presented no evidence of the alleged slave uprising, the suggestion that there might be one in the works cleverly played on the colonists' fears—not only the fear that the slaves might rebel but also the fear that they themselves weren't quite ready to do so.

Dunmore got to hang onto the powder. But, if he was pleased with the way things worked out, that wouldn't last. Nor would peace. Increasingly nervous in the patriot stronghold, in June 1775, Dunmore fled Williamsburg, boarding the HMS *Fowey* in the York River. In the summer of 1776, at almost the same time Virginians were signing the Declaration of Independence, Virginia's last royal governor returned to England.

PUBLIC BUILDINGS

As the capital of Virginia before and during the Revolution, Williamsburg was home to the royal governor and the General Assembly, which was composed of the elected members of the House of Burgesses and the Crown-appointed Governor's Council. Two other institutions that played key roles in American history were also well represented in Williamsburg in the form of Bruton Parish Church and the College of William and Mary.

CAPITOL

It was at the Capitol, as the Revolution approached, that the burgesses debated how best to deal with King George III and Parliament. It was here, in May 1765, that Patrick Henry, angered by the

Stamp Act, delivered his famous speech comparing George III to Caesar and Charles I and warning that the king might meet a similar fate. It was here, in May 1774, that the burgesses resolved to hold a day of "Fasting, Humiliation, and Prayer" to express solidarity with the people of Boston, who were being punished by the British for the Boston Tea Party. And it was here that, in May 1776, Virginia's legislators unanimously declared their independence from England and instructed their representatives to introduce a motion for independence at the Continental Congress. Less than a month later, in Philadelphia, Richard Henry Lee did just that, and Thomas Jefferson went to work on the Declaration of Independence.

The Capitol is shaped like the letter H. The east wing was for the burgesses, who were elected by white, male, Protestant landowners. The west wing had the General Courtroom on the first floor and the Council Chamber on the second. If the burgesses and Council members deadlocked, they met in joint committee in the second-floor chamber connecting the two wings.

The Capitol was also where the General Court met. This was the colony's highest court, presided over by the governor and the twelve members of his Council, who were appointed for life by the king. After 1710, the Court of Oyer and Terminer heard criminal cases here to ease the burden on the General Court.

The original building's foundation was laid in 1701, two years after Williamsburg became the capital of Virginia. Lawmakers moved in in 1704. The Capitol burned in January 1747; after it was rebuilt, the General Assembly met here again in 1753. A generation later, the westward population movement and the fear of attack by British forces resulted in the move of the capital, in April 1780, to Richmond. Soon after, the Williamsburg Capitol began to deteriorate. In 1793, the General Assembly ordered the east end torn down. The west end burned in 1832.

The reconstructed Capitol was based, in part, on a 1928 archaeological dig. The next year, the Bodleian Plate was found at Oxford University. The engraved copper plate, dating back to about 1740, shows in good detail the Capitol, as well as the Governor's Palace and three buildings at the College of William and Mary, providing strong documentation for the original building. Less is known about the appearance of the second Capitol than the first, so the restoration is of the first Capitol, the one ordered by the legislature in 1699. The reconstructed Capitol was completed in 1934.

Near the Capitol is the Secretary's Office. After the Capitol burned in 1747, the Council oversaw the building of a repository for the public records.

PUBLIC GAOL

The Gaol (pronounced "jail") was ordered by the General Assembly in 1701 and was ready in 1704. When the pirate Edward Teach, also known as Blackbeard, was killed in 1718, fifteen of his men were held at the Gaol and thirteen of them subsequently

hanged. The Gaol held assorted criminals, debtors, runaway slaves, the mentally ill, and suspected loyalists during the Revolution. Among those imprisoned here was Lt. Gov. Henry Hamilton of Detroit, also known as the "Hair Buyer," since he allegedly paid his Indian allies for American scalps.

The Gaol itself is thirty feet by twenty feet, and the exercise yard is twenty square feet surrounded by a ten-foot wall. People were held at the Gaol until their trials at the next session of the General Court. Punishment after conviction was generally physical and often harsh, and death by hanging was not uncommon.

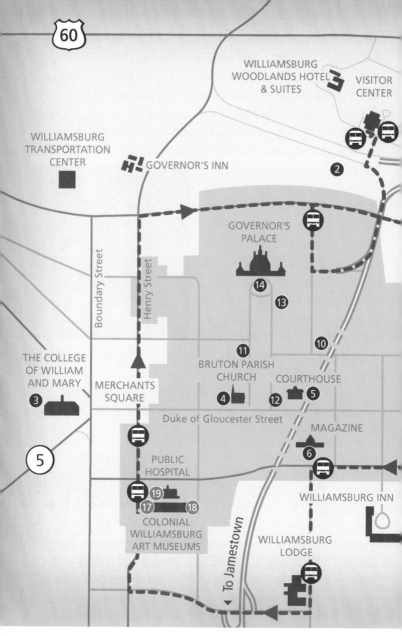

HISTORIC SITES

1. Benjamin Powell House
2. Great Hopes Plantation
3. Wren Building
4. Bruton Parish Church
5. Courthouse
6. Magazine and Guardhouse
7. Raleigh Tavern
8. Capitol
9. Public Gaol
10. Peyton Randolph House
11. George Wythe House
12. James Geddy House
13. Thomas Everard House
14. Governor's Palace
15. Wetherburn's Tavern
16. R. Charlton's Coffeehouse

MUSEUMS

17. DeWitt Wallace Decorative Arts Museum
18. Abby Aldrich Rockefeller Folk Art Museum
19. Public Hospital

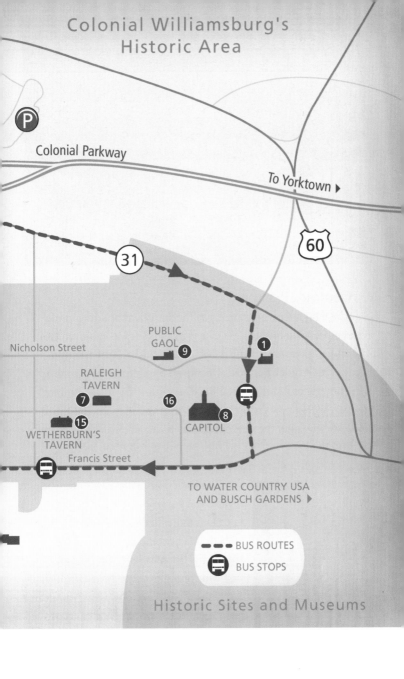

Colonial Williamsburg's Historic Area

P

Colonial Parkway

To Yorktown ▶

60

31

PUBLIC
GAOL

Nicholson Street

9

1

RALEIGH
TAVERN

7

16

8

15

CAPITOL

WETHERBURN'S
TAVERN

Francis Street

TO WATER COUNTRY USA
AND BUSCH GARDENS ▶

- - - BUS ROUTES

BUS STOPS

Historic Sites and Museums

GOVERNOR'S PALACE

The fight over who should pay for this grand building began even before Williamsburg became the capital. It was not until Gov. Alexander Spotswood arrived in 1710 and pushed construction, however, that much got built. He moved into his new residence in 1716, but the building was not finished until 1722. It was paid for basically with a new tax on imported slaves and liquor, and the colonists who paid the new duties may have said "palace" with more derision than respect. On the other hand, it was a fine building. It was extensively enlarged and repaired in 1751 and 1752.

The Governor's Palace was home to seven royal governors, the last of whom, Lord Dunmore, fled for his safety in June 1775. It was next the home of Patrick Henry and Thomas Jefferson, Virginia's first two commonwealth governors. During the siege of Yorktown, it was an American hospital, and 156 Continentals and two women (probably nurses) are buried in the gardens behind the building.

In 1779, the General Assembly passed a bill to move the capital to Richmond, and, that Christmas Eve, the clerk of the House was ordered to send the legislature's records to Richmond. Jefferson left the Palace for Richmond in April 1780. Jefferson did not particularly admire the Palace; in fact, he drew plans for its renovation. He may have had in mind converting it to a private house. "The Palace is not handsome without," he wrote in his *Notes on the State of Virginia*, "but it is spacious and commodious . . . and . . . is capable of being made an elegant seat." That did not happen. The Palace burned to the ground in three hours on December 22, 1781. When reconstruction of the Palace started in 1930, Jefferson's precise drawings helped enormously, as did the Bodleian Plate (the engraving found at Oxford) and extensive archaeological excavations. In 1934, Franklin Roosevelt said it was "born again."

A visit to the Palace still conjures up the power and grandeur of the British Crown. So do the grounds, which include the kitchen, where there are daily demonstrations of the art of colonial cooking.

COURTHOUSE

Built in 1771 in the shape of a T, the Courthouse design was inspired by the second Capitol with its pedimental portico. The por-

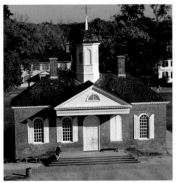

tico was supposed to have been finished with four Ionic columns, but these were not installed. The building was gutted by fire in 1911, and, while it was being rebuilt (the walls had survived), the Williamsburg town fathers ordered four Ionic columns installed. In 1932, Williamsburg and James City County turned

the Courthouse and the green over to Colonial Williamsburg, which returned the building to its original, columnless appearance.

James City County Court sat here, as did Williamsburg municipal (hustings) court. Williamsburg City Council met here for 150 years.

MAGAZINE

Across the street from the Courthouse is the Magazine, built in 1715 in an octagonal format designed by Gov. Alexander Spotswood. He wanted a substantial brick structure to safeguard the colony's arms and ammunition. The Magazine was used to

support Virginia military operations headed by Lt. Col. George Washington during the French and Indian War. With so much gunpowder—at one point, there were more than sixty thousand pounds—a nearby guardhouse and a surrounding wall were added for extra security. They did not help in April 1775 when Lord Dunmore, the last royal governor, sent British seamen to seize the colony's gunpowder. That led to demonstrations, one with Patrick Henry

leading an angry military unit from Hanover County towards Williamsburg to demand gunpowder or payment for it. The anger was calmed and peace restored for the moment, but the seizure helped push Virginia towards revolution.

After the Revolution, the Magazine was, by turns, a private residence, a market, a Baptist church, a Confederate arsenal, a dancing school, a stable, and a small museum called the Powder Horn. The wall around it was torn down in 1856. The Association for the Preservation of Virginia Antiquities bought it in 1889 and kept it from further deterioration, and Colonial Williamsburg restored it to its colonial appearance in 1934–1935.

BRUTON PARISH CHURCH

There was no separation of church and state in colonial Virginia. The Church of England was the established, or state, church, and almost all white colonists in Virginia were members. Bruton Parish was one of the many parishes in the colony. Even before Williamsburg was laid out, when the settlement here was still known as Middle Plantation, an elegant brick church stood just north of the present building. Erected in 1683, the church served the town until it was replaced by a larger one in 1715. Gov. Alexander Spotswood and members of the vestry de-

signed the building. In 1724, the Reverend Hugh Jones described the building as "a large strong piece of brickwork in the form of a cross, nicely regular and convenient, and adorned as the best churches in London."

The church's fine brick and its high rounded doorways and arches gave it a formal and dignified look. "It was a genteel church of aristocracy and gentry," wrote religious historian David Holmes. "Even in the back pews, appearance, clothes, and manners were important."

American Indians in Williamsburg

Most people associate Indians with the narratives of Jamestown and seventeenth-century Virginia, but Native Americans were very much a part of colonial society and present here in the eighteenth century. The aged Attakullakulla, a Cherokee great man from the Over the Hill towns, was no stranger to Williamsburg. As a young warrior of sixteen, he had traveled to Virginia's colonial capital en route to London with Sir Alexander Cumming. Like many of the twenty-odd Cherokee visits in the eighteenth century, the 1730 delegation solidified military and trade alliances between Great Britain and America's Native peoples. Almost fifty years later, Attakullakulla, or the Little Carpenter, as he was called, led an entourage of forty warriors and orators to treat with Virginia's new governor, Patrick Henry. The 1777 visit marked the last formal Cherokee envoy to the capital; the government's move to Richmond in 1780 would begin to close a century of Euro-Indian diplomacy in Williamsburg.

The Cherokee were not the only Native people to be entertained by Virginia's leadership during the colonial period. Thomas Jefferson recalled that, prior to the American Revolution, Indians came to Williamsburg in great numbers for discussions of military alliance, diplomacy, and commerce. Scores of Indian war parties, peace emissaries, and trade brokers had trod down the old Ricahock Path, that is, Duke of Gloucester Street, heading for the House of Burgesses or the Governor's Council. Even before it became the capital in 1699, Middle Plantation, as Williamsburg was then called, was the site of much Euro-Indian exchange. Here, the former palisade ran from Queen's Creek to College Creek, protecting the peninsula's western border. Williamsburg was the scene of the 1677 Treaty of Middle Plantation, a peace agreement that established a tributary relationship between the Crown and the region's indigenous peoples: Pamunkey, Nottoway, Appomattux, Weyanoke, Nansemond, Portabacco, Nanzattico, Manakin, Saponi, and Meherrin. Middle Plantation was also the home to the College of William and Mary, founded in 1693 as a school for the education of English and Indian youth. The Brafferton Indian School was in operation from about 1695–1778 and hosted Native sons from communities including Catawba, Cherokee, Chickahominy, Delaware, Nottoway, Pamunkey, and Wyandot.

Whether treating with the colonial government or visiting their brethren, multiple Indian nations frequented the halls of the Capitol and broke bread in the city's taverns. Hundreds of Catawba stayed in the capital area during the French and Indian War; Shawnee diplomats returned with Virginia's governor to Williamsburg at the conclusion of Dunmore's War; Oneida, Tuscarora, and Mohawk chiefs witnessed the British surrender at Yorktown; dozens of Cherokee joined Washington's Continental army. During the late colonial and Revolutionary eras, Indians were continuously present as groups and individuals as warriors, diplomatic emissaries, traders, translators, students, churchgoers, laborers, slaves, and tradesmen.

Today, the Colonial Williamsburg Foundation's American Indian Initiative offers Native public history on a seasonal basis through partnerships with contemporary communities, such as the Eastern Band of Cherokee Indians.

The church was expanded twenty-two feet to the east in the early 1750s. An organ and the present churchyard wall were added in 1752, and the tower and steeple in 1769.

Bruton Parish Church has been in continuous use since 1715. The church bell, cast at the same foundry as the Liberty Bell, was installed in 1761 and rang for the signing of the Declaration of Independence, the victory over Lord Cornwallis at Yorktown, and the signing of the Treaty of Paris. It still rings today before each service.

After the Revolution, with the end of the favored position of one denomination, membership in Bruton Parish Church declined. In 1840, the old colonial fittings were discarded in favor of more modern ones. The man largely responsible for restoring the sanctuary to its colonial appearance, as well as for restoring the entire Historic Area, was Dr. W. A. R. Goodwin, who became rector in 1903. The church was Goodwin's first experience with a restoration project; later, he would convince John D. Rockefeller Jr. to support the restoration of the entire town. This first project was finished in 1907, in time for the three-hundredth-anniversary celebration of the founding of Jamestown. A more extensive restoration was completed by the Colonial Williamsburg Foundation in 1940.

WREN BUILDING

This building, still in use at the College of William and Mary, takes its name from the famous London architect who designed, among other buildings, St. Paul's Cathedral. In 1724, Hugh Jones, a professor at William and Mary, described the building as "beautiful and commodious, being first modelled by Sir Christopher Wren." In 1693, when King William and Queen Mary granted the college's charter, Wren was surveyor general of the Office of Works in London, and his office was involved in the construction of numerous ecclesiastical buildings. Alas, besides Jones's short comment, there's no real evidence that Wren had a hand in the design, and even Jones added that the building had been "adapted to the nature of the country by the gentlemen there." Still, officially at least, the college has endorsed the Wren connection: when the building was restored in 1931, it was officially dedicated the Sir Christopher Wren Building.

The College of William and Mary

The College of William and Mary is generally agreed to be the second-oldest institution of higher learning (after Harvard) in the nation. Some would argue William and Mary's origins date back before those of Harvard, which was founded in 1636. That argument hinges on tying William and Mary to an earlier college at Henrico near present-day Richmond: In 1619, the Virginia Company provided ten thousand acres for a college to instruct Indian and English boys, which was also the original purpose of William and Mary. Alas, there's not much more than that to connect the two, and, in any case, Henrico never actually opened, a victim of Indian attacks and the Virginia Company's near-bankruptcy.

Statue of Lord Botetourt in front of the Wren Building.

William and Mary's origins precede those of Williamsburg itself. In May 1691, when the area was still known as Middle Plantation, the Reverend Dr. James Blair, the bishop of London's representative in Virginia, set off for England to ask King William and Queen Mary to grant a charter for a college. Blair had the support of Virginia's governor and General Assembly, and, on February 8, 1693, the king and queen granted the charter. It called for establishing "a certain Place of universal Study, a perpetual College of Divinity, Philosophy, Languages, and other good Arts and Sciences." In August 1695, the foundation was laid for the school's first building.

William and Mary contributed a great deal to the education of future Revolutionaries. It was here that George Washington received his surveyor's license. Thomas Jefferson arrived in 1760, and his closest college friend, John Page, reported that Jefferson "could tear himself away from his dearest friends, to fly to his studies." Jefferson's biographer Dumas Malone described the future president's education as one that "anybody in any age might envy." James Monroe arrived at William and Mary in 1774; John Marshall in 1780. Washington's continuing connection to the college—he became chancellor in 1788—lasted until his death in 1799.

The statue in front of the Wren Building, originally ordered for the Capitol but later moved to the college, is of Norborne Berkeley, Baron de Botetourt. Botetourt was royal governor of Virginia until his death in 1770. Behind the Wren Building is the Sunken Garden, conceived by Jefferson.

Today, though William and Mary still has "College" in its name, it's actually a small university. Many campus theater and dance performances are open to the public. So is the Muscarelle Museum of Art, whose paintings include works by Jasper Cropsey, Rembrandt Peale, Isabel Bishop, Georgia O'Keeffe, Jacob Lawrence, and Hans Hofmann.

TAVERNS AND COFFEEHOUSE

Taverns and coffeehouses played a key role in the social and political life of the eighteenth century, and four of Williamsburg's taverns—Christiana Campbell's Tavern, Chowning's Tavern, Shields Tavern, and the King's Arms Tavern—continue to serve twenty-first-century diners (see pages 241–243). The King's Arms Tavern today retains its pre-Revolutionary name, but, with customers like George Washington, it's no surprise that in Revolutionary times the name was changed to the Eagle Tavern.

R. CHARLTON'S COFFEEHOUSE

R. Charlton's Coffeehouse, which opened in 2009, was the first full reconstruction on Duke of Gloucester Street for fifty years. Based on extensive archaeological research and built with eighteenth-century materials and methods, it is also the only eighteenth-century coffeehouse in America. It's an exhibition site, not a working coffeehouse, though tours do include samples of coffee, tea, or hot chocolate made in the style of the times.

The caffeinated drinks (and the location near the Capitol) undoubtedly fueled heated political discussions. Ten years before the Revolution, the Coffeehouse played a role in a major demonstration of resistance to British taxation. In 1765, a crowd furious about the Stamp Act threatened George Mercer, the chief distributor in Virginia of the hated stamps. In a letter of October 30, Lt. Gov. Fauquier recounted how, while he was sitting on the Coffeehouse porch with members of his Council, he had to pull Mercer from the street. The crowd did not disperse, so Fauquier walked Mercer through "the thickest of the people who did not molest us; tho' there was some little murmurs."

The building, alas, was replaced by a larger Victorian house in the late nineteenth century. Archaeologists and architectural historians studied the site and other evidence not just to plan the reconstruction of the Coffeehouse but also to understand how Charlton created a setting that attracted such gentry as Washington and Jefferson as well as successful merchants. Fragments of wine bottles and peacock bones suggested what was available to drink and eat at the Coffeehouse.

In 1767, Charlton advertised in the *Virginia Gazette* that his coffeehouse was now a tavern, which meant that he would offer lodging, perhaps in an attempt to generate more business. By 1770, however, the tavern had closed.

RALEIGH TAVERN

The Raleigh Tavern is named for Sir Walter Raleigh, a favorite of Queen Elizabeth. Raleigh was such a favorite that, in 1584, Elizabeth granted him an exclusive patent to colonize America. Alas, Raleigh fell out of the queen's favor and also that of King James, who imprisoned him in the Tower of London and eventually put him to death.

The tavern opened about 1717 and eventually became a social and political center of the colony. When royal governors Botetourt and Dunmore dissolved the House of Burgesses, the members walked to the Raleigh Tavern and reassembled in the Apollo Room. It was also in the Raleigh Tavern that Patrick Henry, Thomas Jefferson, Jefferson's brother-in-law Dabney Carr, and the Lee brothers, Richard Henry and Francis Lightfoot, agreed to establish as a "committee of correspondence" to keep other colonies aware of Revolutionary developments in Virginia.

At other times, the Raleigh Tavern was the site of balls and other entertainments that attracted gentry as well as wealthy merchants. George Washington often noted in his diary, "Dined at the Raleigh." Citizens threw a lavish dinner here for Peyton Randolph in 1774 after he was named the first of Virginia's delegates to the opening Continental Congress, and Patrick Henry's troops honored him with a dinner here in 1776. Students from the College of William and Mary founded the Phi Beta Kappa

Society in the Apollo Room in 1776.

As the Revolution approached, the Raleigh opened its doors to the less wealthy. A Continental soldier who attended a wedding there described "silk and flannel dancing hand in hand." When Lafayette came back for his final tour of America in 1824, the party was at the Raleigh. In December 1859, the tavern burned to the ground. It was rebuilt between 1928 and 1932 with the aid of two illustrations, archaeological information about the foundation, and a 1771 inventory.

And now a bit of colonial gossip. When he was a twenty-year-old student at William and Mary, in October 1763, Thomas Jefferson danced with Rebecca Burwell, whom he called Belinda, in the Apollo Room. He intended to propose, but it did not go well. By his own account to a friend, his proposal or attempt at it came out as "a few broken sentences, uttered in great disorder, and interrupted with pauses of uncommon length." Jefferson, who would prove to be a brilliant writer, never got any better as a speaker. The next year Belinda married Jacquelin Ambler, the treasurer of Virginia, and they had five daughters. The second daughter, Mary Willis Ambler, married John Marshall, future chief justice of the United States, who called her Polly. The marriage made Jefferson's fair Belinda Marshall's mother-in-law. Jefferson and Marshall were lifelong political enemies. Is that the reason? No, but it makes for intriguing speculation.

WETHERBURN'S TAVERN

Like other colonial tavern keepers, Henry Wetherburn offered lodging as well as food and drink. His tavern was so popular that he added a twenty-five-by-twenty-five-foot "great room," which was used for meetings and balls. The building, one of the Historic Area's original eighty-eight, was meticulously refurnished based on a detailed inventory of Wetherburn's estate. Extensive archaeological research also aided the restoration. Among the archaeologists' finds were about fifty wine bottles filled with cherries. The bottling may have been done to preserve the cherries or to make brandied cherries.

Homes

The charm and elegance of eighteenth-century Williamsburg can best be seen through its homes. The homes also offer insights into how the Revolution tore apart Virginian families, such as the Randolphs.

Peyton Randolph House

John Randolph, born in Virginia, was knighted for service to the Crown. He was widely regarded as the colony's most distinguished lawyer. He served as clerk and Speaker of the House of Burgesses, attorney general, and treasurer of the colony. He and his wife, Susannah, had three sons and one daughter. When Sir John died in 1737, he left his Gloucester County plantations to his oldest son, Beverley, who eventually moved there and became a planter. Sir John left his Williamsburg home to his widow for life and then to his second son, Peyton. He also left his law library to Peyton, "hoping he will betake himself to the study of the law." Peyton and his younger brother, John, both studied at the College of William and Mary and then went to the Inns of Court in London to study law. Peyton returned to become attorney general, was elected to the House of Burgesses, and became Speaker of the House in 1766. Brother John became attorney general, was an adviser to royal governors Francis Fauquier and Lord Botetourt, and was a confidant of Lord Dunmore.

As the Revolution approached, John was a leading loyalist, Peyton a leading patriot. Although both brothers were political moderates and hoped to remain British, when that was no longer possible, Peyton chose the Revolution, John the Crown. John, his wife, Ariana, and their daughters sailed for England in 1775, and he has been known since as John the Tory. At least one of Peyton

Randolph's slaves, his wife's personal maid Eve, also chose the British side, fleeing to British troops when they occupied Williamsburg in 1781. One estimate is that 25 to 30 percent of Virginians were loyalists, compared to 50 percent of New Yorkers and only 10 percent of colonists in New England.

A month before the first Continental Congress in 1774, Virginia's leading Revolutionaries met at Peyton Randolph's house to determine what course they would take and then went to Philadelphia. Randolph, described as open and cordial, was unanimously elected president of the Congress. When he returned, the Williamsburg militia rode out to greet him. Admirers in Williamsburg called him the "father of his country" (this before that title settled on George Washington). Randolph was elected to the presidency of the second Congress but was called home to preside over the House of Burgesses. In 1775, shortly after he returned to Philadelphia, he had a stroke and soon died. A side note: Thomas Jefferson, his cousin, bought Randolph's law library, and, combined with his own collection of books, they became the nucleus of the original Library of Congress.

Betty Randolph and her house servants continued to live in the house after her husband's death. She had to deal with the British occupation in 1781; then her home was used as the headquarters of the comte de Rochambeau before the siege of Yorktown. George Washington's headquarters before Yorktown was the George Wythe House, a block or so west across Palace Green.

The Peyton Randolph House is restored, and original paneling exists in several rooms. There is a marble mantle in the dining room that was installed in the early 1750s when Peyton Randolph expanded the original 1718 house. The house is, in fact, three connected buildings. Behind the house, Colonial Williamsburg tradespeople have reconstructed what was probably Williamsburg's most extensive domestic compound, including a covered-way kitchen, laundry, dairy, and granary.

GEORGE WYTHE HOUSE

George Wythe (pronounced "with") was from plantation society, born in Elizabeth City County, now part of Hampton, in 1726. He was admitted to the bar in Virginia when he was twenty and became a noted classical scholar. In 1754, he was elected to the House of Burgesses from Williamsburg and was acting attorney general while Peyton Randolph was away. He was a friend of royal governors Francis Fauquier and Lord Botetourt, served as clerk of the House from 1769 to 1775, and worked for independence, republican values,

and the authority of the courts. He signed the Declaration of Independence, was elected Speaker of the House of Delegates of the independent Commonwealth of Virginia in 1777, and was one of three judges in 1778 on Virginia's High Court of Chancery. With Jefferson and Edmund Randolph, Wythe revised the laws of the Commonwealth. In short, he knew everyone who was anyone though he's best remembered today for teaching law and having a strong influence on Thomas Jefferson. Jefferson and his family stayed at Wythe's house for several weeks in 1776. Jefferson called Wythe "my faithful and beloved Mentor in youth, and my most affectionate friend through life." After the war, Wythe became the first professor of law at the College of William and Mary, the first at any college in the country, where he taught John Marshall, the fourth and longest serving chief justice of the United States.

George Wythe was poisoned in Richmond in 1806, almost certainly by his grandnephew George Wythe Sweeney, who lived with him. Sweeney was a deadbeat who ran up debts and wrote checks for money he did not have. He expected a substantial inheritance from his granduncle, so he poisoned him. Wythe lived long enough to write Sweeney out of his will, which, incidentally, gave all his books to Jefferson. Sweeney was never punished. Why? The witness against him could not testify. She was the cook, Lydia Broadnax, a slave Wythe had freed, and a black person could not legally testify against a white person.

Unlike many houses, including Randolph's, Wythe's was not the result of a series of additions but conceived as a whole in the 1750s. It was, in George Wythe's time, considered the finest private home in Williamsburg.

JAMES GEDDY HOUSE

This L-shaped building was the home of silversmith James Geddy Jr., whose shop is right beside the house. James's father and brothers operated a gunsmith/foundry behind the house (see page 163). James Geddy Sr. opened the gunsmith/foundry after emigrating from Scotland. When James Sr. died, the gunsmith/foundry continued under the ownership of James's older brothers, William and David.

Interpreters today focus on the effect of the Revolution on both James Geddy Jr.'s silversmith business and on his family. James Geddy Jr. was a patriot, and his political position took a heavy toll on his business and home.

Children visiting the Geddy House today will get a sense of what life was like for the five Geddy children living during this period, both inside the house where the young Geddys were taught to read, write, and play the spinet and outside where there are games and toys—such as hoops and sticks, mancala, and quoits—similar to those the Geddy children would have enjoyed.

Thomas Everard House

Built by John Brush in 1718, the house takes its name from Thomas Everard, who acquired the property about 1755 and served as mayor of Williamsburg and clerk of the York County Court. Guests learn about Everard's contributions to Williamsburg and the Revolution.

Benjamin Powell House

Benjamin Powell, once a wheelwright, became a successful builder. Along with Randolph, Wythe, and others, he was a member of a committee that enforced an embargo on selected British goods in 1774. Today, there are activities for children in the house.

Great Hopes Plantation

At Great Hopes Plantation, costumed tradespeople and interpreters are re-creating a typical Virginia farm. It's a very different world from the large and more famous plantations, but most Virginians—whites of modest means and free and enslaved black people—lived at places like Great Hopes. Depending on when you visit, you may find carpenters working on construction projects with eighteenth-century tools or farmers tending their livestock and crops.

Historic Trades

"If you listen as you stroll the streets of Colonial Williamsburg's Historic Area, you hear the pulses of work," says director of Historic Trades James Gaynor. "There is the whoosh of a sharp plane surfacing a board and the rustle of silk as a gown is sewn. Axes thump into wood, and anvils ring to hammer strikes."

The men and women at work are practicing eighteenth-century trades while also sharing their knowledge. Some of what's made in the Historic Area is available for sale at the Prentis Store (see page 253).

GUNSMITH AND FOUNDRY

The Geddy family included gunsmiths, silversmiths, founders, and blacksmiths. At the Geddy site today, you can watch gunsmiths making rifles, fowlers, pistols, tomahawks, and knives using only eighteenth-century methods and tools. Working alongside them, founders cast brass, bronze, silver, and pewter into a variety of useful and ornamental items such as shoe buckles, spoons, candlesticks, and pipe tampers. William and David followed in their father's footsteps and became gunsmiths; James Jr. became a silversmith. They supported the patriot cause during the war. David joined the army and was last heard of at Valley Forge. William did contract work casting cannonballs and making swords.

BLACKSMITH

The James Anderson Blacksmith Shop was rebuilt on the original foundation in the late 1980s using colonial tools, techniques, and materials. It was originally built in the 1770s. During the Revolutionary War, Anderson served as the public blacksmith to repair muskets, swords, and bayonets and provide tools and hardware to the Commonwealth of Virginia and the Continental army. Tradesmen at the shop also made

and repaired household goods, farm implements, and tools and made iron goods for other trades. Still today, when the iron is hot and, therefore, soft enough, smiths carry it from a coal-fired forge to an anvil and hammer it into shape.

PRINTING OFFICE, POST OFFICE, BOOKBINDERY

William Parks was a postmaster and printer, jobs that often went together in the colonies. He published the first issue of Virginia's first newspaper, the *Virginia Gazette,* on August 6, 1736. The *Gazette* included both domestic and foreign news as well as advertisements. Parks also did the official printing of Virginia's laws for the House of Burgesses.

As the Revolution approached, Parks's successors antagonized some patriots, who in 1766 convinced William Rind to open a competitive newspaper, also called the *Virginia Gazette.* Rind's widow, Clementina, continued the business after his death. In 1774, Rind printed Thomas Jefferson's *A Summary View of the Rights of British America.* In 1775, a Scotsman named Alexander Purdie printed a third newspaper, once again called the *Virginia Gazette.* For awhile, Williamsburg printers published three newspapers, all with the same name.

Today, pressmen work the press much as their eighteenth-century predecessors did. A typesetter sets each metal letter by hand. The composed type is mounted on the wooden printing press. The printer uses two stuffed leather ink balls to spread ink onto the type. Using the lever of the press, he then forces dampened paper onto the inked type, printing the page.

Across the courtyard, at the Bookbindery, pages of books are folded, pressed, sewn, and trimmed. In the eighteenth century, these were largely record-keeping books for the government, churches, plantation owners, and merchants. The covers of some books were made of fine leather that was tooled, stamped, and decorated with designs, sometimes in gold leaf.

Today in the Post Office, located above the Printing Office, cards and letters are still hand-canceled. A variety of prints, books, stationery supplies, and maps are offered for sale.

Milliner

The Margaret Hunter Shop is a milliner's shop. Typically a woman, a milliner made and sold fashionable clothing accessories for the family, such as shirts, shifts, cloaks, caps, aprons, and stomachers. Milliners also trimmed hats, made baby clothing, mended fans, and did fine laundry. Eighteenth-century customers could also buy fashionable imported items like tea, shoes, stockings, jewelry, fine fabrics, dolls, and walking sticks. Currently, this shop also is home to the tailors, who make men's suits and ladies' riding habits, and the mantua-makers, who make women's and children's gowns.

Silversmith

The Golden Ball carries on the tradition of James Craig, who established his business here by 1767, at the sign of the golden ball. Craig advertised silverwork, jewelry, toys, fine cutlery, mourning rings, watches, and spectacles. George Washington was one of his customers. Today, the master silversmith and his journeymen and apprentices use eighteenth-century skills such as raising, forging, chasing, and engraving to produce hollowware such as drinking vessels, bowls, and sauceboats as well as gold and silver jewelry.

APOTHECARY

Drs. William Pasteur and John Galt diagnosed, prescribed, compounded medications, and performed surgery. Today the Pasteur & Galt Apothecary Shop features a large collection of antique drug jars and medical equipment and a staff devoted to researching medical history.

WIGMAKER

The King's Arms Barber Shop houses the wigmaker (also known as perukemaker, from the French word for wigs). In the eighteenth century, the shop also provided barbering and hairdressing services to ladies and gentlemen. Wigmaker Edward Charlton kept careful records of his business and his customers from 1752 to 1792, so we know that Patrick Henry, Thomas Jefferson, Peyton Randolph, and George Wythe were among his clientele.

CABINETMAKER

At Hay's Cabinetmaking Shop, Anthony Hay (later keeper of the Raleigh Tavern) and others made furniture that matched the styles in London. Benjamin Bucktrout, who took over as master of the shop in 1767, advertised a wide range of woodworking services, including the manufacture and repair of harpsichords. The shop also advertised—this was not unusual among cabinetmakers—coffins and funeral services.

BRICKYARD

At the Brickyard, brickmakers mold, dry, and fire bricks that are used for reconstruction work in the Historic Area. During the summer months, guests, especially the younger sort, enjoy stomping around in the clay to help mix it. In colonial times, this work was usually done by slaves, indentured servants, and unskilled free laborers.

OTHER TRADES

Tradespeople at the Taliaferro-Cole Shop weave and dye a variety of fabrics. Down the street, the Shoemaker's Shop represents one of ten or more that operated in eighteenth-century Williamsburg and produced ready-made shoes for gentlemen in a variety of sizes

and styles or made shoes and boots to measure.

Before there were forklifts and pallets, goods were most often stored and transported in wooden barrels like those made by the coopers at the Ludwell-Paradise Stable. Not only are these barrels strong and tight, but they can be rolled to wherever they have to go. Wheelwrights at the Elkanah Deane Shop produce wheels, wheelbarrows, carts, and freight wagons. Basketmakers demonstrate their trade on the Wythe property, and carpenters work at Great Hopes Plantation and at building sites around town and practice their joinery in the Ayscough House. Foodways cooks working at the Governor's Palace and Peyton Randolph kitchens daily prepare foods using eighteenth-century recipes and, on special occasions, demonstrate the arts of brewing, ice cream making, and chocolate making.

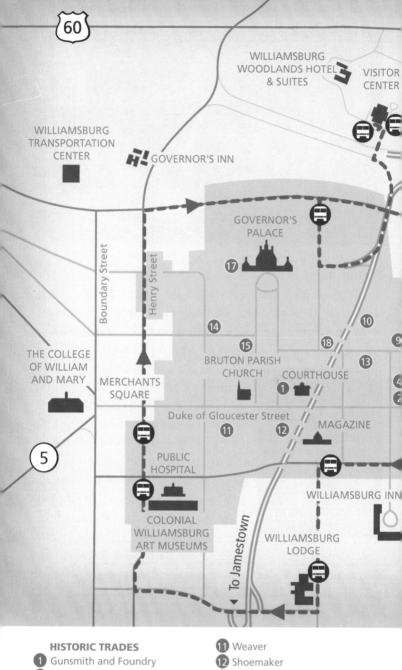

HISTORIC TRADES

1. Gunsmith and Foundry
2. Printer
3. Blacksmith
4. Bookbinder
5. Milliner and Tailor
6. Silversmith
7. Apothecary
8. Wigmaker
9. Cabinetmaker
10. Brickmaker
11. Weaver
12. Shoemaker
13. Cooper
14. Wheelwright
15. Basketmaker (on George Wythe property)
16. Joiner
17. Foodways (in Governor's Palace kitchen)
18. Foodways (in Peyton Randolph kitchen)

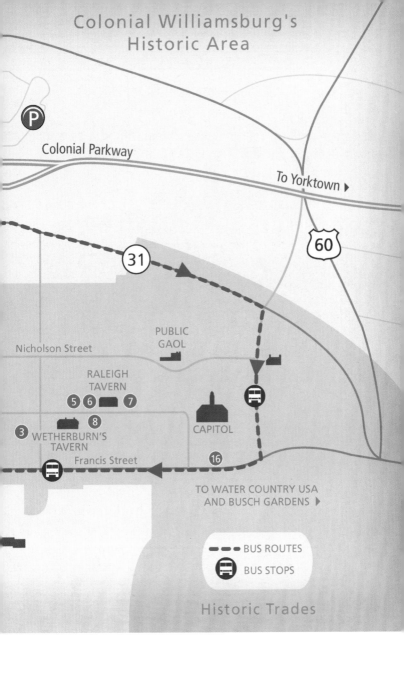

Colonial Williamsburg's Historic Area

Gardens

"No occupation is so delightful to me as the culture of the earth, and no culture comparable to that of the garden." So wrote Thomas Jefferson, and so would agree all those who have delighted in the gardens of the Historic Area. Boxwoods abound, sometimes precisely trimmed and other times billowing naturally, along with dogwoods, redbuds, magnolias, catalpas, and fruit trees.

The many and sundry gardens of the Historic Area are always changing, not just because of the passage of time but also because new research and techniques have revealed more about the gardens of the eighteenth century. Yet, there's no question, as Gordon Chappell and M. Kent Brinkley wrote in *The Gardens of Colonial Williamsburg*, that "these gardens capture the spirit and character of the finest eighteenth-century colonial gardens."

Governor's Palace

The most famous of Williamsburg's gardens, in colonial times and today, are those of the Governor's Palace. Originally envisioned by Gov. Alexander Spotswood in the early 1700s, they were so extensive and extravagant that members of the General Assembly, noting that the gardens were being paid for by the public, complained to Spotswood about the expense. The Bodleian Plate, a copperplate found in 1929 at Oxford University, which shows the property in good detail, helped the landscape architect re-create the Palace gardens.

In the formal gardens surrounding the Palace ballroom are pleached arbors in which the branches of American beeches interlace to form a tunnel that provides shade and privacy. In the spring, thousands of brightly colored tulips fill the central flower beds, followed by summer annuals. Topiaries trimmed into various shapes are also striking. The fruit garden features cordoned apples and pears and espaliered plums, peaches, and figs. The trees are trained to grow along supports such as a frame of locust poles or a wall.

One of the Palace's most popular features is a maze of yaupon hollies planted next to the original mount. While there is no documented evidence that a maze existed here in the 1700s, records indicate that the areas overlooked by mounts were planted as mazes. Mounts were popular features in the gardens of sixteenth-century English aristocrats and served to insulate an icehouse in the ground beneath.

On the west side of the Palace are Spotswood's "falling gardens," terraces dug by the governor's slaves. A canal, once criticized by burgesses as a high-priced "fish pond," is one of the most bucolic spots in Williamsburg. The overhanging trees, quaint bridges, and naturalistic plantings are a striking contrast to the rigid geometrical patterns of the Palace's more formal gardens.

OTHER GARDENS

Among the Historic Area's other popular gardens is that of the John Blair House. Its beds are filled with a mix of herbs. Colonists grew herbs such as lavender and rosemary to scent cosmetics. Other herbs such as santolina and tansy were strewn over the floors of colonial homes to improve the smell, crucial in an era when people bathed infrequently. Wormwood was rubbed on furniture to repel flies. You can find it growing behind Wetherburn's Tavern.

The Taliaferro-Cole garden, like many in the Historic Area, is colorful year-round, with spring bulbs, summer perennials, and flowering trees and fruiting shrubs. The knotty look of the pollarded sycamore trees near the pasture is the result of a pruning technique called pollarding. The garden's picket fence is also unusual.

The Prentis garden illustrates how much can be made with just a typical half-acre lot. Red cedars mark the back of the property, pomegranates screen the garden on one side, and rectangles edged by yaupon hollies are accented with red buckeye trees underplanted with common periwinkles.

A Prentis family diary and planting lists help garden historians interpret gardening techniques at the Colonial Garden and Nursery.

Colonial Garden and Nursery

At the Colonial Garden and Nursery on Duke of Gloucester Street, opposite Bruton Parish Church, you can see gardeners at work using colonial-style rakes and wheelbarrows. You can also see some eighteenth-century solutions to age-old problems. There are the bee bottles, for example, which draw bees to a sugar solution and then trap them inside, and the bell glass, a miniature greenhouse used to protect delicate plants from the cold.

Museums

The entire Historic Area is a living museum. Colonial Williamsburg's treasures can also be seen in two traditional art museums at the DeWitt Wallace Decorative Arts Museum and the Abby Aldrich Rockefeller Folk Art Museum. Both are at the site of the Public Hospital.

Public Hospital

The hospital, which opened in 1773, was the first public institution for care of the mentally ill in the British colonies. Exhibits trace the evolution of attitudes and treatments over the next century.

DeWitt Wallace Decorative Arts Museum

Research on the household furnishings of eighteenth-century

Virginia progressed markedly during the first fifty years of the restoration. Initially, the exhibition buildings were furnished mostly with ornate eighteenth-century objects from Great Britain, New England, and the mid-Atlantic region. As information about the interiors of Williamsburg buildings emerged, it led to the acquisition of more regionally appropriate antiques, including furniture and other objects fashioned in nearby areas. Many of the antiques and works of art acquired earlier were ultimately replaced in the exhibition buildings, leaving a large collection of furniture and decorative household wares in storage. What was needed was a place to display them.

Enter DeWitt and Lila Acheson Wallace, cofounders and publishers of *Reader's Digest*. The couple admired what John D. Rockefeller Jr. had done and donated more than $14 million to build a museum for Colonial Williamsburg's treasures. The collections today include American and British firearms, ceramics, paintings, furniture, textiles, clothing, maps, tools, and metal objects from 1600 to 1830.

The Masterworks gallery presents a cross section of the finest objects in the collection. Among them is a handsome clock from about 1700 made by Thomas Tompion for King William III (after whom Williamsburg was named). It was owned by all succeeding British monarchs through Queen Victoria. Tompion's clocks were sophisticated engineering accomplishments—this one required

winding only every three months and did not require resetting for leap years.

A Japanned high chest illustrates a decorating technique that was popular among wealthy New England consumers who were captivated by imported objects and fashions from the Far East.

Charles Willson Peale was probably the best-known artist working in America during the Revolution. His portrait of George Washington at Princeton, where Americans won a key battle, is a rare survival and of monumental size. Like many Americans, Peale was a staunch patriot and believed that the heroes of the new country were as worthy of celebrating as kings and queens.

A dozen other galleries at the DeWitt Wallace Museum feature changing themed exhibits that explore aspects of eighteenth-century history, fashion, and technology. The variety and range of objects include utilitarian stoneware jugs, ornamental porcelain, pewter plates and silver tureens, coins and currency, fine furniture, musical instruments, and a great deal more.

ABBY ALDRICH ROCKEFELLER FOLK ART MUSEUM

Along with her husband, John D. Rockefeller Jr., Abby Aldrich Rockefeller played an important role in shaping Colonial Williamsburg's educational mission. She was a pioneer collector of modern art and American folk art, and she observed a strong aesthetic relationship between the two. She gave the principal portion of her folk art collection to Colonial Williamsburg in the late 1930s, and, in 1957, it became the nucleus of this country's first museum devoted to the subject.

Folk artists usually had little or no training in fine arts practices and techniques (although many were aware of such art and artists).

Their work tends to show less a formal style and more a personal and creative use of line, color, form, and decoration. For these reasons, folk art often seems highly idiosyncratic and occasionally abstract. The Williamsburg collection, spanning the eighteenth century to the present, includes furniture, metal wares, pottery, paintings, drawings, needlework, quilts, carvings, and sculpture in a variety of media.

The art world has not always recognized many folk artists. Ulysses Davis, for example, displayed his carvings in his barbershop rather than in a gallery or museum. Edward Hicks was trained as a carriage and sign painter though his most famous work was a series of paintings known as the "Peaceable Kingdom." While these images strike us as yearnings for harmony in our lives, they also reflect the years of discord within the Society of Friends in America (Quakers) that resulted in a schism in the late 1820s.

Hicks is one of the most famous folk artists represented in the Williamsburg museums, which own the largest single collection of his work. But, there's more in the museum in the way of painted images, including portraits, landscape and farmscapes, still lifes,

watercolors, and pen and ink pictures. There are also signboards and sculptures whose purposes were once commercial, but which also once filled American streets and buildings with the type of surprises you're unlikely to find today.

The Peaceable Kingdom of the Branch by Edward Hicks, 1822–1825.

Bassett Hall

In 1927, Abby Aldrich and John D. Rockefeller Jr. acquired eighteenth-century Bassett Hall as a residence and furnished it with choice pieces from their collections of antiques and American folk art. Unlike the rest of the Historic Area, which embodies the late colonial period, the house and grounds have been restored to look precisely as they did in the late 1930s and 1940s, when the Rockefellers made it their Williamsburg home.

Visiting
Yorktown

YORKTOWN

WATERMEN'S
MUSEUM

RIVERWALK
LANDING

YORKTOWN
VICTORY CENTER

17

WATER STREET

YORK RIVER

MAIN STREET

BALLARD STREET

NELSON
HOUSE

YORKTOWN
VICTORY
MONUMENT

MAIN STREET

BALLARD STREET

COLONIAL
PARKWAY

YORKTOWN BATTLEFIELD

INTRODUCING YORKTOWN

You remember that Jamestown has two places? Yorktown has three: Yorktown Battlefield, the town of Yorktown, and the Yorktown Victory Center. Yorktown Battlefield and portions of the historic town, which is a real town where nearly 250 people live, are run by the National Park Service, a federal agency, which also manages (with Preservation Virginia) Historic Jamestowne. As was the case for Jamestown, the Park Service's site is where history, in this case the winning of the final major battle of the American Revolution, actually happened. The Yorktown Victory Center is run by the Jamestown-Yorktown Foundation, the state agency that also runs Jamestown Settlement. The Yorktown Victory Center is a museum with indoor galleries and outdoor interpretive areas where people in period costume show you what life was like, in this case, during and after the war. There are visitor centers at both the battlefield and the Victory Center, with the former's serving as one for the town as well.

If you like to walk, Yorktown is your place. There is a walkway from the visitor center at the battlefield along the York River to the Victory Center—from one end of Yorktown to the other—one and a half miles in all. There are walking tours of the battlefield and walking tours of the town. If you don't want to walk, the free Yorktown Trolley circles the village between April and October. It is also easy to drive around Yorktown with ample parking throughout the town and at both visitor centers.

The battlefield is at the east end of town; the town is in the middle on an east-west line; the Victory Center is at the west end. If you keep the York River in front of you (north), it's hard to get lost or confused. From town, remember that the battlefield is right, the Victory Center is left. The Colonial Parkway is south of town, roughly parallel to the river, and it will take you to all three sites.

Colonial Parkway

Besides its historic significance, Colonial National Historical Park also surrounds one of America's most beautiful drives. The park's twenty-three-mile Colonial Parkway is designated an All-American Road by the U.S. Department of Transportation, one of only thirty-one nationwide. You can see many of the park's nearly nine thousand acres from the Colonial Parkway, which connects the three points of the Historic Triangle.

Though proposed as early as 1909 by Williamsburg City Council, the idea of the parkway didn't gain momentum until the 1920s, as Williamsburg's restoration got under way. In 1930, President Herbert Hoover signed legislation to preserve what were then known as America's "sacred shrines." They sorely needed preserving: Jamestown had reverted to farmland and marshland and part of the Yorktown battlefield was a golf course. The legislation called for a scenic roadway linking Jamestown, Williamsburg, and Yorktown.

It took twenty-six years to complete the twenty-three-mile road.

One major problem was how to route the parkway through Williamsburg. The National Park Service advocated heading east and south of the city since this would have balanced the York River section with views of the James River. But this route would have crossed the property of Bassett Hall, then the summer home of the Rockefellers. The Colonial Williamsburg Foundation opposed the plan.

In 1936, Dr. W.A.R. Goodwin, the man who'd initially convinced the Rockefellers to restore Williamsburg, suggested building a tunnel underneath the city. Rockefeller's first reaction was that he'd "never heard of a crazier idea in my life." Goodwin, however, had not lost his knack for getting Rockefeller to see the merits of his ideas, and, in 1940, construction began. Though plagued by cave-ins that damaged structures along its route, construction of the tunnel was completed within two years. The section of the parkway that includes the tunnel opened in 1949, and the entire parkway in 1957, just in time for Jamestown's 350th anniversary.

Paved to look like a country road, the parkway provides dramatic open views of the James and York Rivers as well as marshes, ponds, fields, woods, and coastal bluffs. In June and July, you can see the Yorktown onion in bloom. Yorktown is one of the few places in America where you can see its long stem and wine-colored head.

YORKTOWN
BATTLEFIELD

YORK RIVER

REDOUBTS
9 AND 10

YORKTOWN
BATTLEFIELD
VISITOR CENTER

MOORE
HOUSE

Colonial Parkway

238

238

Goosley Road

Surrender Road

BATTLEFIELD TOUR

238

BATTLEFIELD TOUR

ALLIED
ENCAMPMENT
TOUR

DRIVING TOUR

ALLIED ENCAMPMENT TOUR

What to See at Yorktown Battlefield

www.nps.gov/colo
757-898-3400

The National Park Service has preserved four thousand acres of battlefield. The best place to start (and park) is the Visitor Center.

Visitor Center

The Visitor Center has a fifteen-minute film about the siege; offers tours, maps, and programs; and has exhibits, including two of George Washington's tents: his office tent, the inner sanctum where most of the general's business was conducted, and a portion of his dining marquee, where Washington and his staff took meals. The dining marquee is displayed so that, rather than seeing it from outside, you step inside the walls. Places that advertise "Washington slept here" have nothing on you; you are where he ate, planned, conferred, gave orders, and won.

The Visitor Center also has the cannon and battle flag sur-

rendered by the British army at the end of the siege, as well as the "Lafayette cannon," a piece of artillery used by the British army during the siege and recognized by the famed French general when he returned to America forty-three years later.

Earthworks

Standing on the field outside the museum, you can see the earthworks Cornwallis's men built. In the distance, you can see what's known as the second allied siege line. French and American troops began building this on October 11. To finish the line, the allies had to take two small British earthen forts that blocked their way—Redoubts No. 9 and No. 10. These are just to your left as you face the second allied siege line. On the night of October 14, French and American troops attacked. Within thirty minutes, both redoubts were in allied hands. The opposing lines were now only four hundred yards apart, allowing the allies to fire point-blank on the British position. Two days later, Cornwallis tried to flee across the York River, but there was no escape.

DRIVING TOUR

A self-guided driving tour of the battlefield is marked with large, easily seen grey directional signs with red arrows. There are actually two tours that are connected. The first, which takes you through the battlefield sites chronologically, is seven miles long. The second, which covers the encampment areas of the American and French armies, is nine miles. Warning, caution, and all that: the tour alternates between park roads, with lower speed limits and a minimum of traffic, and public highways, with higher traffic speeds and volume. Do not get so caught up in what you are seeing that you ignore traffic, traffic signs and signals, bicyclists, joggers, and drivers doing what they sometimes do even though it makes no sense.

On both routes, there are parking areas with signs telling what happened nearby. The driving tours alternate between open battlefield and forested areas that are enormously attractive. What you need to remember is that the Continental, French, British, and German troops were not riding through the woods in modern comfort. It was October, and it was a cold October in Virginia. Siege guns, cannons, and mortars rarely stopped. The fighting troops at Yorktown did not know if they would die, or how, or when. Smallpox and other diseases were rampant and were far more likely to kill the troops than cannon fire. One of the stops on the nine-mile tour is the French cemetery where about fifty French troops are buried, or tradition accepts that they are. The stop before the cemetery is Washington's headquarters, where Washington's tent, now on display in the Visitor Center, was pitched in 1781.

At some of the stops, Surrender Field, for instance, there are parking lots and walking trails to sites farther off the road. The Moore House is at the easternmost point on the tour. It was here that two officers from each side met to negotiate surrender terms on October 18, 1781. It was Cornwallis who suggested Augustine Moore's house as the negotiating site. With 80 percent of Yorktown's buildings in ruins due to the bombardment, there was no choice but to go beyond the siege lines to find a location for the meeting.

A seventy-five-minute narrated tour of the battlefield is available at the Visitor Center for a nominal fee.

WHAT TO SEE IN THE TOWN OF YORKTOWN

TOWN

As you walk around the village, which is about fourteen square blocks, remember that historic sites are mixed in with private residences. This is both a historic village and the current county seat where people live and work.

There are about a dozen buildings in Yorktown that are original or restored to their eighteenth-century appearance. Some now house shops or restaurants. The Nelson House may be the most impressive. It has been restored and is operated by the National Park Service and is open for visitation.

Thomas Nelson Jr., a signer of the Declaration of Independence, was governor of Virginia at the time of the siege of Yorktown. As commander of the Virginia militia, Nelson targeted his own house when he suspected that it was being used as Cornwallis's headquarters. It was hit several times, and some of the shot marks can still be seen on the exterior bricks, but the house survived, one of the few targeted buildings that did. The walls are eighteen inches of solid brick.

The first building to be restored by the National Park Service was the Moore House. The Moore House, where the British surrender was negotiated, is about one and a half miles outside of town to the east.

Across Read Street from the Nelson House is the Custom House, erected in 1721 as a storehouse by Richard Ambler. Ambler collected duties from ship captains during Yorktown's heyday as a port. The site is currently owned and operated by the Daughters of the American Revolution.

On Main Street, you will find galleries, antique shops, and restaurants. Just off Main Street is Grace Episcopal Church, built about 1697 of marl, a deposit of compressed marine shells and clay that occurs around Yorktown. The church's communion silver was made in 1649.

WATERFRONT

You can head down to the York River via either Ballard Street or the Great Valley Road. Along Water Street, which fronts the river, you'll find Cornwallis's Cave, where, we are told, the British commander survived part of the siege. That is a legend, and there are some interesting "haunted cave" stories to go with the legend—sounds of crying and sobbing and despair. In reality, Cornwallis sat out the siege in a bunker located approximately a quarter mile south. The site today is marked along a trail called Tobacco Road in a ravine between the Yorktown Victory Monument and the Visitor Center. There are no haunted bunker stories.

Along the waterfront are restaurants and a retail area, Riverwalk Landing. There's also the Watermen's Museum. The term *waterman,* which refers to commercial fishermen as well as others who work on water, is used only on the Thames River in England and around the Chesapeake Bay. Watermen had a role in the siege of Yorktown, acting as pilots for the French fleet.

Yorktown Victory Monument

On a rise of land at the east end of town is the Monument to Victory and Alliance, popularly known as the Yorktown Victory

Monument. When the Continental Congress at Philadelphia learned of General Washington's victory at Yorktown, it passed a resolution on October 29, "That the United States in Congress assembled, will cause to be erected at York, in Virginia, a marble column . . ." It did not say when. The cornerstone was laid October 19, 1881, at the opening of the Yorktown centennial celebration.

The four sides of the base have inscriptions, including brief stories of the siege, of the alliance with France in 1778, and of the peace treaty with England in 1783. A podium above the base carries the sculpture of thirteen female figures (the colonies), hand in hand, dancing on the words, "ONE COUNTRY—ONE CONSTITUTION—ONE DESTINY." The column, which rises from the podium, includes, among other emblems, thirty-eight stars, one for each state in 1881. Atop the column is Liberty herself, which was set in place on April 12, 1884. The memorial is ninety-eight feet tall and is inside what would have been Cornwallis's defensive line.

A ninety-eight-foot column on a high point of land was bound to attract lightning sooner or later, and, on July 29, 1942, Liberty was so badly damaged that the sculpture had to be replaced. Lightning protection was added to the monument, the whole thing was thoroughly cleaned and repaired, a new Liberty was sculpted, and the Yorktown Victory Monument was ready for Yorktown Day, the annual observance of the American victory, in October 1957. Lightning struck again in 1990, damaging the figure somewhat— hand and torso. Repairs were made and the lightning rods improved. Lightning has not struck again.

The Sunken Fleet

Though Cornwallis surrendered on land, the American victory at Yorktown was largely won on water. The British forces in Virginia, indeed throughout North America, depended on the British navy for supplies, reinforcements, and support of all kinds. On September 5, near Cape Henry (the same point where the settlers bound for Jamestown first came ashore), a British fleet under Adm. Thomas Graves faced a French fleet under Adm. François-Joseph-Paul de Grasse. They fought to a standoff, though some British ships suffered damage to their masts and rigging. On September 9, an additional French squadron arrived, and soon thereafter Graves withdrew to New York for repairs. Without Graves, Cornwallis was trapped.

Still, Cornwallis had a few warships and some merchant and transport vessels. He scuttled, or intentionally sank, twelve of the merchant vessels to form a barrier to thwart an attack from the river. That left him sixteen ships, enough to carry his troops across the York River in three waves. On October 16, Cornwallis attempted to flee. He ordered the first wave of troops onto the small boats. They landed across the York River. Around midnight, though, a violent storm forced the second wave of troops back to Yorktown. Realizing the situation was hopeless, Cornwallis ordered more of the ships sunk so that they wouldn't fall into American or French hands. Allied shelling also damaged the small fleet.

And so the British fleet came to rest on the bottom of the York River. "At a small distance from the shore were seen ships sunk down to the Waters Edge," wrote St. George Tucker in his journal. "Further out in the Channel the Masts . . . of some might be seen, without any vestige of the hulls."

After the surrender, the French salvaged some of the ships or their fittings, and later locals and others grabbed more, but the brunt of the fleet remained underwater. In 1934 and 1935, a diving expedition organized by the National Park Service, the Mariners' Museum in Newport News, and Newport News Shipbuilding recovered thousands of objects including bottles, ceramics, and cannons. This was, however, before the invention of scuba equipment, so there was much the divers couldn't get to or see.

In 1981, divers were able to explore more thoroughly, and they found nine ships. One, later identified as the *Betsy*, was well preserved by thick silt. Originally a collier, or coal carrier, the thirty-ton schooner had been used to carry supplies and troops. Divers brought up a wealth of artifacts, including saucers and bowls, ink bottles, a wig curler, musket balls, shoes, rat skulls, and part of the ship's rigging. They even found a coin under the main mast, where shipwrights traditionally placed one to ensure good winds.

Toward the end of the excavation, divers found a rectangular opening carefully chiseled through the hull. Below it was an empty toolbox and scattered carpentry tools, indicating that the *Betsy* was among the ships Cornwallis had scuttled.

"The shipwreck remains from the Battle of Yorktown constitute one of the most diverse and extensive deposits of shipwrecks in North America dating from the colonial period," concluded naval historian John O. Sands. "Including both naval and merchant vessels, of varying size, with considerable supporting documentation available, it is an unparalleled resource for the study of eighteenth-century shipping and life."

An exhibit at the Yorktown Victory Center includes a re-creation of surviving sections of the *Betsy*, a scale model of the ship, and many of the artifacts found on board.

British ship during 1780 battle (detail)
by Irwin John Bevan (1852–1940).

WHAT TO SEE AT THE YORKTOWN VICTORY CENTER

www.historyisfun.org

1-888-593-4682 or 757-253-4838

*T*he indoor galleries and outdoor interpretive areas at the Yorktown Victory Center complement the sights at the battlefield and in the town of Yorktown. A one-story brick building welcomes you.

ROAD TO REVOLUTION

Start your tour down the Road to Revolution, a time line and exhibits along an open-air walkway that gets you into the museum and gives you a good and brief story of events leading to the Revolutionary War. To the right, along a handrail, there are quotations from people of the Revolutionary period—blue signs for Continentals, red for British—and data. You start in 1750 when the population of the colonies reached one million; you end in 1776 when America declared independence.

On your left along the walk are open pavilions providing background to the events that led to the Revolutionary War. You can learn a little just by walking past and reading the biggest signs or learn more by stopping and reading more. Each has one wall and a roof, so stopping creates some comfort in bad or hot weather. Each has a single-word title. One is "Treaty," which is about the treaty of

1763 that ended the French and Indian War, which started in 1754 even though war was not declared until two years later. Essentially, the war was the fight between the French and the British for control of the Ohio Valley and what was then the American frontier. This war, which was expensive, led to friction between the American

colonies and England over who would pay for it and how.

Another pavilion is titled "Taxes." In a series of acts, starting with the Stamp Act, the British parliament imposed taxes on the colonists to require them to pay a share of the cost of the French and Indian War. The British thought that only fair since the

American frontier had been secured. The Americans resented taxation without representation. Notice that a section of the wall, where all the information is posted, has fallen out. The wall at the "Treaty" node is solid, and, at a node called "Tea," the wall is partially split. The condition of the walls is a representation of the political relationship between England and America, and, by the time of the Boston Tea Party, a reaction to the Tea Act of 1773, that relationship was in serious trouble. The war started in April 1775 in Massachusetts, a year before the Declaration of Independence, when British troops were sent from Boston to seize arms caches at Lexington and Concord. Like the French and Indian War, this war was not declared; it just was.

GALLERIES

In the museum, you can walk through a series of exhibits. An introductory gallery portrays the Declaration of Independence as a radical document that inspired decisive action. One of the objects exhibited is a rare broadside of the Declaration of Independence from July 1776 before a handwritten copy on parchment was signed by members of Congress.

In the Witnesses to Revolution gallery, there are ten figures representing a cross section of real people whose lives were affected by the war. As each is lit in turn, a recorded voice speaks. The words are from written records—a diary, a couple of petitions for pensions after the war, a book, letters home, and other original sources. Among the ten are three women, two slaves, and an American Indian. A private from Rhode Island kept a diary and notes that he and some

buddies killed a dog and that he was grateful for a small piece of the dogmeat to eat. Matthew Patten, a farmer, sent two sons off to war and then helped neighboring women whose husbands had gone to fight for independence get their crops in. One of his sons died of smallpox while in the army.

Throughout the museum, there are graphics of key events leading to the siege of Yorktown as the two sides converged on the port town. British general Charles Cornwallis came to Virginia from the Carolinas, and American general George Washington from New York and New Jersey. Washington had sent Lafayette to Virginia earlier, but his force was pitifully small. Maps illustrate troop movements—who did what, who went where. The abbreviated version is that both sides were in place on September 28, 1781, although the French and Americans did not fire their first salvos until October 9.

Objects on display include a portrait of Cornwallis and a two-hundred-year-old original map of the area drawn by a Frenchman, including a handwritten legend. You can also see the two flintlock pistols that Lafayette gave to the American doctor who treated him when he had pneumonia. These are not replicas or models; these are Lafayette's pistols.

Next, you'll again hear from real people, this time people who lived through the siege—the wife of an American soldier, a French artillery officer, an English naval officer, and a German officer. All four kept diaries. The German's was published by Princeton University. The "witness" theme continues in *A Time of Revolution*, an eighteen-minute film set in an encampment during the siege of Yorktown that dramatizes the musings and recollections of an array of individuals.

A ramp leads downstairs to the Yorktown's Sunken Fleet display. Cornwallis ordered British ships lashed together and scuttled—intentionally sunk—close to shore either to prevent an assault from French vessels in the river or to prevent the ships from being captured by the Americans and French. The display features artifacts from the British supply ship *Betsy*, the most extensively studied of the wrecks. In the 1980s, archaeologists built a cofferdam around the *Betsy*; a five-minute video shows the work being done. The ship is still in the river, but the center has re-created a section of it. Clever use of light makes it appear underwater. The two-masted coal carrier was 73 feet long and 23 feet wide with a capacity of about 175 tons. Though a collier, the *Betsy* served in the war as a troops transport and a floating workshop. Artifacts recovered from the *Betsy* include everyday items of officers, crew, and craftsmen and reveal what life was like at sea.

Back upstairs, you'll come to the Legacy of Yorktown: Virginia Beckons. The United States of America was not fully formed the day Cornwallis and his troops surrendered. For one thing, the war was not formally concluded for two more years. For another, we were thirteen individual nation-states, loosely bound in a confederacy. Exhibits here focus on the public debate over what kind of government the United States would have. Drafted in 1787, the Constitution was formally adopted in 1788 and the Bill of Rights in 1791. On display you can see Constitutional Convention delegate Pierce Butler's edited draft of the document and a Boston newspaper with headlines relating Virginia governor Edmund Randolph's dislike for the proposed Constitution.

A common misunderstanding about colonial Virginians is that everyone fell into two classes—rich plantation owners and

African slaves. The Virginia Beckons exhibit sheds light on the actual composition of Virginia. It covers immigration from before 1607 until about 1830 and shows where the settlers came from and where they settled in Virginia. The Scots-Irish, for example, came through Philadelphia, headed south, and settled the Shenandoah Valley.

Also inside the museum is a children's discovery room where kids can try on clothes of the colonial period.

CONTINENTAL ARMY ENCAMPMENT

Outside is an encampment of Continentals, as American troops were then known. It is not any specific unit at any specific place. The tents and furnishings are replicas, and costumed interpreters depict the daily life of American soldiers near the end of the war. Visitors can explore soldiers' tents and learn about eighteenth-century medical practices and the role of the quartermaster in managing troop supplies. Fairly regularly, one of the Continentals fires his musket off to one side, a great favorite of young guests. The musket is loaded with powder, so there is a satisfying bang and a good deal of smoke, but, since it is not loaded with a ball, no projectile comes out of the barrel. It's a lot safer that way. For a bigger bang and more smoke, interpreters fire a cannon daily from March through December.

REVOLUTION-ERA FARM

After you tour the encampment, you can walk through a re-created eighteenth-century farm, complete with house, kitchen, tobacco barn, crop fields, and herb and vegetable garden, all showing how many Americans lived at the time of the Revolution. Costumed interpreters are available to answer questions. What is going on will depend on the season. In the two hundred-plus years since the siege of Yorktown, *how* farming is done has changed completely; *what* is done season by season has hardly changed at all.

Tobacco

From the colony's early days to the Revolution, tobacco played a key role in Virginia history.

That tobacco turned out to be the basis of the colony's success was at least ironic given the attitude of the man after whom Jamestown was named. King James hated smoking. In *A Counterblaste to Tobacco*, which James himself wrote in 1604, he described the habit as "lothsome to the eye, hatefull to the Nose, harmefull to the braine, dangerous to the Lungs."

The king's distaste, however, did not dissuade Pocahontas's husband, colonist John Rolfe, from transplanting to Virginia the sweet-scented Spanish tobacco grown in the West Indies. (The variety cultivated by Indians was "poore and weake, and of a byting taste.") Exactly where he planted his first crop is a matter of dispute. Some historians think it was at Jamestown, others that it was upriver at Henricus.

Unlike the colonists' earlier ventures, among them vineyards, silkworms, and glassblowing, Rolfe's sweet-scented tobacco was an immediate hit. By the end of 1615, the colony exported twenty-three hundred pounds of leaves. By 1617, Samuel Argall described even the streets as planted with tobacco. By 1619, John Pory reported, "All our riches for the present doe consiste in Tobacco." By 1628, total exports were more than a half million pounds; by 1700, they were more than twenty-eight million pounds. The chance to plant tobacco drew new colonists, and tobacco plantations soon spread up the James River and across the colony. Planters bragged about the quality of their leaves the way winemakers would their grapes. With coins and paper money rare, tobacco was literally the currency of the colony.

Though tobacco made many Virginians rich, King James wasn't the only dissenter. Virginia Company officials worried that colonists weren't planting anything else because of the "overweening esteeme of theire darlinge Tobacco." Indeed, the dangers of a one-crop economy became clear in the 1660s when the market became glutted and tobacco prices plummeted. From then on, market cycles drove many a planter deep into debt. "Can it be otherwise," asked George Washington in 1765, "than a little mortifying to find, that we, who raise none but Sweet-scented Tobacco . . . shoud meet with such unprofitable returns?" Washington eventually planted wheat instead.

By the eve of the Revolution, Virginians owed British merchants almost two million pounds. This debt was not only mortifying but also, in the opinion of some historians, a cause of the planters' Revolutionary zeal. In the early twentieth century, Charles Beard and others argued that large landowners' rhetoric about freedom and liberty was largely a justification for their real motive: to avoid paying their debts. More recently, historians like Woody Holton have argued that debt was one of several economic and other factors pushing the planters toward revolution.

Most historians today would reject a strictly economic explanation. The planters' talk of liberty was more than a cynical ploy; the American Revolution was propelled by a genuinely revolutionary ideology. Still, there's no denying that tobacco and politics were intertwined. "Certainly the endless discussions of increasing debts, depressed tobacco prices, and shortages of currency that occupy so large a part of the surviving correspondence of Virginians suggests the possibility of a link between economic conditions in the colony and the Revolutionary movement," stated historian Thad Tate.

If tobacco deserves some of the credit for the Revolution, it also deserves some of the blame for slavery. It was not nearly as easy to grow tobacco as its early enthusiasts claimed. The plants demanded attention throughout the growing season; they had to be weeded and wormed and suckered and topped; then the leaves had to be stripped and cured. These were much more labor-intensive processes than those for corn or wheat. At first, landowners did this work themselves or alongside white servants, but gradually they came to depend on black slaves.

"It is a culture productive of infinite wretchedness," wrote Thomas Jefferson. "Those employed in it are in a continued state of exertion beyond the powers of nature to support."

While You're Here

The James River plantations, John Marshall's and Patrick Henry's homes, Jefferson's Monticello: the Historic Triangle is surrounded by history. And there's more than history nearby, so we've also included other top attractions, from the coasters of Busch Gardens to the coast of Virginia Beach. Most are less than an hour's drive, and none are much more than two hours away.

INSIDE THE TRIANGLE

The Historic Triangle offers a chance to experience not only seventeenth- and eighteenth-century history but also twenty-first-century thrills.

BUSCH GARDENS

www.buschgardens.com
800-343-7946

Situated on 350 fun-filled acres, Busch Gardens boasts more than fifty rides and attractions, ten shows, and plenty of food and shopping. The Sesame Street–themed children's area draws the park's younger visitors. More daring guests can brave the Griffon, a floorless dive coaster that ascends over two hundred feet. Each year,

Busch Gardens adds a little something new to its line-up. You can now enjoy a simulated motion adventure ride that propels visitors on a journey through Europe and a nightly celebration hosted by each country that makes up Busch Gardens. The celebration culminates in a parkwide pyrotechnic display. The park lights up for the holiday season with Christmas Town: A Busch Gardens Christmas.

Busch Gardens is dedicated to the conservation and preservation of wildlife through numerous educational programs and shows. Jack Hanna's Wild Reserve offers an up-close look at such species as gray wolves, American bald eagles, and lorikeets.

Water Country USA
www.watercountryusa.com
800-343-7946

Just three miles west of Busch Gardens is Water Country USA. Guests can plunge into fun at the mid-Atlantic's largest water play park, featuring a 1950s and '60s surf theme. Water Country USA has forty-three acres of pools, children's play areas, lazy rivers, water rides, and a new dive show. On Rock 'n Roll Island, you can plunge down nearly six hundred feet of body slides, relax on the seven hundred–foot lazy river, and play in a nine thousand–square–foot pool. Or take a break and just soak up the sun in one of nearly fifteen hundred lounge chairs throughout the park.

Go-Karts Plus
www.gokartsplus.com
757-564-7600

This amusement park features bumper boats, bumper cars,

miniature golf, the Disk 'O' thrill ride, Water Wars, children's rides, an arcade, and, of course, four go-cart tracks.

PRESIDENTS PARK
www.presidentspark.org
757-259-1121
800-588-4327

The park features eighteen- to twenty-foot busts of forty-three U. S. presidents. The statues were sculpted by artist David Adickes.

RIPLEY'S BELIEVE IT OR NOT!
www.WilliamsburgRipleys.com
757-220-9220

The museum has more than three hundred exhibits, including a five-hundred-pound gorilla made entirely of nails, a genuine shrunken head, and a 4-D theater.

WATERMEN'S MUSEUM
www.watermens.org
757-887-2641

At Yorktown Beach, the museum interprets the maritime heritage of the Chesapeake Bay through exhibits, educational programs, living history, and traditional boat-building projects.

WILLIAMSBURG WINERY
www.williamsburgwinery.com
757-229-0999

Virginia's largest winery offers tours and tastings. Lunch is served at the Gabriel Archer Tavern.

JAMES RIVER PLANTATIONS

The grand plantations that line the James River, many off scenic Route 5 between Williamsburg and Richmond, were homes to many of Virginia's—and America's—leaders.

BERKELEY PLANTATION
www.berkeleyplantation.com
804-829-6018
888-466-6018

Here, in December 1619, a band of Englishmen landed, fell to their knees, and thanked God for their safe arrival. The "instructions" sent with them from England said that "the day of our ships arrivall . . . shall be yearly and perpetualy kept holy as a day of

thanksgiving to Almighty god." One year and seventeen days before the Pilgrims arrived in New England, these Virginia settlers had already celebrated the first "Thanksgiving" in America. Each year on the first Sunday in November, Thanksgiving is celebrated with a living history program.

Unlike the Pilgrims' Thanksgiving, Berkeley's did not commemorate a friendship with Indians. In 1622, Indians attacked and killed most of the inhabitants. After that, the settlement fell into disrepair.

In 1691, Berkeley was acquired by the Harrison family, and, in 1726, Benjamin Harrison IV built the Georgian mansion that still stands. The house was the birthplace of Benjamin Harrison V, a signer of the Declaration of Independence, and of William Henry Harrison, the ninth president of the United States.

It was at Berkeley that William Henry Harrison composed his inaugural address, the longest in presidential history. Harrison caught pneumonia while giving the speech and died a month later. William Henry Harrison gave the longest inaugural address and stayed in office the shortest length of time of any president. His grandson, another Benjamin Harrison, became the twenty-third president.

After the Harrisons lost control of the plantation in the 1840s, it changed hands several times. During the Civil War, the plantation was occupied by Gen. George McClellan's Union troops. President Lincoln visited Berkeley on two occasions during McClellan's encampment.

Also at Berkeley, Gen. Daniel Butterfield composed the familiar tune "Taps," first played by his bugler, O. W. Norton.

The original 1726 manor house has a unique collection of eighteenth-century antiques. Five terraces of gardens offer views of the James River.

Next door to Berkeley is Westover Plantation. Though the house is closed to the public most of the year, the grounds are open and worth a visit. The mansion, like Berkeley, is Georgian. It's famous for its elaborate doorway.

Shirley Plantation
www.shirleyplantation.com
804-829-5121

Shirley Plantation was first settled in 1613, just six years after Jamestown and seven years before the Pilgrims reached Plymouth Rock. The present mansion was begun in 1723 and finished in 1738. The carved pineapple on the roof is a symbol of hospitality, and guests here included George Washington, Thomas Jefferson, and other prominent Virginians. Anne Hill Carter, the mother of Confederate general Robert E. Lee, was born at Shirley, and, in 1793, she married Henry "Light-Horse Harry" Lee in the mansion's parlor.

The house holds Hill and Carter family portraits and some of the family's elegant furniture and silver. Its most famous feature is its

"flying" staircase, which rises three stories with no visible means of support. Nine of the plantation's eighteenth-century brick outbuildings survive, four of which form a Queen Anne forecourt. Shirley Plantation is owned, operated, and lived in by the eleventh generation of the Hill-Carter family.

SHERWOOD FOREST
www.sherwoodforest.org
804-829-5377

Our tenth president, John Tyler, was unpopular with many in his own Whig party, who had supported William Henry Harrison as their presidential candidate and never intended Tyler to be anything more than vice president. (Harrison died just thirty days after his inauguration.) One prominent Whig, Henry Clay, referred to Tyler as an outlaw and dubbed his plantation "Sherwood Forest" after the home of the most famous outlaw of his time. Tyler liked the name and it stuck.

The house, which was started about 1730, is notable for being the longest frame house in America. At 301 feet, it's one foot longer than a football field though only one room deep. The house suffered only minimal damage during the Civil War since the Union soldiers who occupied the plantation were under orders to protect the homes of ex-presidents even though this particular ex-president was at that time a member of the Confederate Congress.

The grounds include an overseer's house, a smokehouse, a wine house, a kitchen, and a laundry—all evidence of the extent to which plantations like Sherwood Forest were self-sufficient during the eighteenth century.

NEWPORT NEWS

Some say Newport News was named after Christopher Newport, who commanded the three ships that reached Jamestown in 1607. Others trace it to William Newce, who arrived from Ireland in 1621. Either way, Newport News has plenty to see and is just a few miles east of Williamsburg.

MARINERS' MUSEUM
www.mariner.org
757-596-2222

In December 1862, just months after battling the CSS *Virginia* (formerly the USS *Merrimack,* when it was in Union hands) in the waters of Hampton Roads, the USS *Monitor* sank in a storm near Cape Hatteras. In 1973, the wreck was located and became America's

Monitor and Merrimac, 1st Fight Between Ironclads, chromolithograph by J. O. Davidson, 1886.

first National Marine Sanctuary in 1975. Much of what was recovered is now at the Mariners' Museum.

Looking at the *Monitor*'s reconstructed turret, you can imagine the durability and power of the ship. The *Monitor* and the *Virginia* were the first two ironclad ships to battle. Though the battle ended as a draw, it changed the course of naval history. After March 1862, no country aspiring to naval superiority would ever again depend on a wooden battleship.

The *Monitor* makes up only a tiny fraction of the museum's extraordinary collection that includes 35,000 maritime artifacts from around the world. The museum has, to be precise, 127 small crafts, 340 pieces of deck and steering equipment (including anchors and steering wheels), 2,335 pieces of furniture and galley equipment, 1,586 sailors' uniforms or other belongings, and 1,451 pieces of navigational equipment, including rare timepieces, chronometers, compasses, quadrants, sextants, and lighthouse equipment. For those who prefer their boats in miniature, there are almost 1,800 model ships, including 16 exquisitely detailed masterpieces by the artist-carver August Crabtree. There are also 374 carved figureheads and name boards and 11,392 paintings, drawings, prints, watercolors, and engravings.

Virginia Living Museum
www.thevlm.org
757-595-1900

Here's a chance to get a closer look at the animals that live in or around the region's backyards—raccoons, foxes, deer, skunks, opossums, and more than two hundred other native Virginians. What makes them all the more appealing is that they can be seen in their native habitats. You can also look underwater in the Chesapeake Bay exhibit and underground in the limestone cave exhibit. And a coastal plain aviary showcases birds that breed in Virginia or migrate through the state. Travel the universe in the state-of-the-art digital planetarium theater. Learn how to build, live, and garden green in the Living Green House and Conservation Garden.

Endview Plantation
www.endview.org
757-887-1862

Lee Hall Mansion
www.leehall.org
757-888-3371

En route from Williamsburg to Yorktown in 1781, Virginia militiamen stopped at the home that later became known as Endview. But these two sites are primarily for those interested in the Civil War when Endview served as a Confederate hospital and Lee Hall was headquarters for Confederate generals John Bankhead Magruder and Joseph E. Johnston.

Hampton

Just east of Newport News is Hampton, whose museums offer a chance to learn about military, African-American, Indian, and space and aviation history.

Fort Monroe
www-tradoc.Monroe.army.mil/museum
757-788-3391

Look beyond a thirty-two-pound gun and through one of the openings in the old stone walls of Fort Monroe. You'll see the moat surrounding the fort and, beyond that, the Chesapeake Bay. It's a view that can only be called commanding.

For almost two hundred years, Fort Monroe has controlled the entrance to the James and York Rivers. It's the largest stone fortification ever built in the United States. Among those stationed here was

Robert E. Lee, who, as a second lieutenant in the army between 1831 and 1834, was responsible for excavating the moat and finishing the outer fortifications. It was when Lee was outside these walls, however, that Fort Monroe gained its greatest fame. During the Civil War, the fort remained in Union hands; indeed, it was one of the few forts in the South never captured by the Confederates.

The fort's greatest contribution to the war effort was more ideological than military. In 1861, three escaped slaves sought refuge here. When their owner demanded them back, Maj. Gen. Benjamin Butler ruled that they were contraband of war. After that, thousands of other slaves sought sanctuary in what became known as "The Freedom Fort." Butler's decision was one of the first public acknowledgments that the Civil War was, at least partly, a war against slavery.

The fort's nickname held many ironies, not the least of which was that it was built in part by slave labor. Another was that it was the place where Confederate president Jefferson Davis was imprisoned after the war. His cell was casement number two, a stark enclave built to house a gun, not a person. It's furnished now, as then, only with Davis's bed and a table. On the table is a Bible and an Episcopal prayer book, the only books Davis was allowed during his two years there.

After touring the casements, take a walk on top of them. The fort's grassy roof offers more expansive views than its narrow embrasures. Just make sure to keep a close eye on kids and pets—the drop-off from the roof to the moat is steep and dangerous. A pet cemetery on the roof provides an unintentional reminder.

Hampton University Museum
www.hamptonu.edu/museum
757-727-5308

For the rulers of many African nations, the "seat of power" is no figure of speech. Instead, it's an actual seat, the most important piece of furniture in the nation. And no one but the owner—usually the king—is allowed to sit on it. Some of these intricately decorated seats, such as an Asante stool from Ghana and a Kuba stool from the Congo, are among the thirty-five hundred African artifacts and works of art at the Hampton University Museum.

The museum also has a remarkable collection of paintings and sculptures by African Americans. Works by such artists as Aaron Douglas and William H. Johnson exemplify the explosion of talent that came out of the Harlem Renaissance. And there's a significant collection of art inspired by the Civil Rights movement. These include works by Jacob Lawrence and Elizabeth Catlett. Probably the most famous painting in the museum dates back to 1893, however. This is Henry O. Tanner's *The Banjo Lesson*.

The museum has an impressive collection of about seventeen hundred Native American objects, including examples of basketry, beadwork, quillwork, painting, pottery, and textiles. This collection was largely an outgrowth of the school's early commitment, between 1878 and 1923, to educate Native Americans alongside African Americans.

Virginia Air and Space Center
www.vasc.org
757-727-0900

NASA has its launching pads at Cape Canaveral, its mission control in Houston. But, much of the research that led to the moon and beyond took place at NASA's Langley Research Center in Hampton. It was at Langley that researchers developed the technology for Mercury, Gemini, Apollo, Skylab, and the space shuttle. And, it was at Langley that America's astronauts once underwent their training and simulated landings.

Tightened security means you can no longer enter Langley itself. Instead, head to the Virginia Air and Space Center in downtown

Hampton. This building, which resembles a bird in flight, serves as Langley's visitor center as well as Hampton Roads' answer to the Smithsonian. Here you can see a meteorite from Mars and a rock from the moon. The latter, which arrived via the 1972 Apollo 17 mission, is three billion years old.

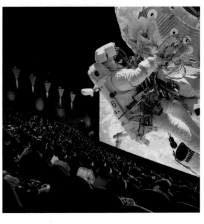

But, it's the spacecraft most people come to see. The museum has the actual Apollo 12 command module that carried three men around the moon in 1969 (and which was the only part of the Apollo vehicle that returned to earth). Here, too, are the Apollo lunar excursion module simulator (LEMS) that astronauts used to practice landing on the moon and a replica of the Viking Mars lander that took the first color photos showing that the "red planet" really is red (the result of oxidized iron).

There are also plenty of airplanes representing Langley's contributions to air travel closer to earth. All the aircraft are suspended from the museum's ceiling, and they can be viewed from three different levels.

Norfolk

From Hampton, take the tunnel under Hampton Roads and you'll come to Norfolk, a city with a range of attractions for those with an interest in the military, past and present. The Chrysler Museum of Art provides an excellent starting point for a tour of nearby Ghent, a neighborhood of eighteenth- and nineteenth-century homes, most restored to their earlier grandeur. Colley Avenue is Ghent's liveliest, with many restaurants, bars, boutiques, and trendy shops.

Chrysler Museum of Art
www.chrysler.org
757-664-6200

Take a look at George Caleb Bingham's nineteenth-century rendition of *Washington Crossing the Delaware*. At first glance, it seems to be just another version of the familiar image. But, look closely: instead of the traditional rowboat, Washington is in a Missouri River flatboat. Bingham has set the scene in the Midwest, perhaps

to appeal to his fellow mid-westerners or perhaps just to give it a fresh look. Washington is also on a horse, a heroic but hardly wise pose to take on an open raft.

The point is that the art at the Chrysler is worth a careful look.

The collection includes thirty-five thousand objects spanning five thousand years, from ancient Asia, Africa, and pre-Columbian through the present. The impressionist gallery is especially remarkable. There are works by Cézanne, Degas, Gauguin, Monet, and Renoir, among others. The glass galleries include an extensive collection of Louis Comfort Tiffany's glassworks, including windows, lamps, tiles, and just about anything else you'd need to furnish a home.

The museum also operates two of Norfolk's historic homes, the Moses Myers House and the Willoughby-Baylor House (which houses the Norfolk History Museum).

MacArthur Memorial
www.macarthurmemorial.org
757-441-2965

"Old soldiers never die. They just fade away." So said Gen. Douglas MacArthur in his April 1951 address to Congress, just a few

days after President Harry Truman had relieved him of his command. At the MacArthur Memorial, where the general is buried, his memory has definitely not faded away. Here you can see the medals, uniforms, flags, swords, personal papers, and battle souvenirs of one of the military's most colorful and controversial figures.

Nauticus and USS Wisconsin
www.nauticus.org
757-664-1000

Norfolk's is the world's largest naval base. There's room for eighty ships, though many are spread around the globe. For the sake of security, you can't go on the ships or even enter the base, except on a tour. To board an actual battleship, head downtown to Nauticus, where the USS *Wisconsin* is berthed. Though only about half the length of a modern aircraft carrier, she still carried twenty-seven to twenty-nine hundred men during World War II and fifteen hundred during the Gulf War. The interior passageways form such a maze

that one sailor spent three days looking for a friend in another division. He finally wrote him a postcard that said, "Meet me on the deck beside Turret No. 3 at noon."

At Nauticus, a museum of maritime science, you will also find more than 150 hands-on exhibits, many of which appeal to kids. You can practice knots, build a Lego ship, simulate drilling for undersea oil, or touch a whirling tornado. Make split-second naval battle decisions in the Aegis theater. Both the USS *Wisconsin* and Nauticus are part of the National Maritime Center.

NORFOLK BOTANICAL GARDEN
www.norfolkbotanicalgarden.org
757-441-5830

With more than 155 acres, you may want to board the trams and boats that take you through the garden. To stop and smell the flowers, of course, you're best off on foot. The garden is actually a series of themed gardens. For example, the Bicentennial Rose Garden (dedicated in 1976) has more than 2,300 rose plants representing 260 varieties. The Flowering Arboretum has 336 different flowering trees. No matter what the season, something's in bloom.

VIRGINIA ZOO
www.virginiazoo.org
757-441-2374

Lions, elephants, kangaroos, meerkats: the zoo has more than 350 animals representing 110 species. Prairie dogs scurry in and out of their burrows. In the African section, animals roam freely within a system of moats separating them from guests. These settings provide glimpses of the animals' natural environments and of more natural behaviors.

PORTSMOUTH
www.portsmouthva.gov/tourism
757-393-5111

Just a quick ferry ride from Norfolk, Portsmouth's Olde Towne has a remarkable collection of colonial, Federal, Greek revival, Georgian, and Victorian homes, all restored to their eighteenth- and nineteenth-century splendor. On the edges of Olde Towne are a number of museums worth a stop. The Naval Shipyard Museum features models of many ships. The Lightship Museum is an actual lightship, which once guided ships through dangerous waters. The Virginia Sports Hall of Fame has memorabilia from state greats. And the Children's Museum of Virginia, with more than ninety hands-on exhibits, is where kids can step into a giant bubble or take control of the equipment at a construction site.

VIRGINIA BEACH

Just north of Virginia Beach is Cape Henry, where, three weeks before they reached Jamestown, the English colonists first landed in America. From this same site, 174 years later, you could see British and French ships in the battle that sealed the fate of the British army at Yorktown.

Today, Virginia Beach is the place to go for surf and sand. The liveliest stretch is between about 14th and 26th Streets. During the season, there are almost always concerts or street performers juggling or riding unicycles or giving puppet shows. If you prefer things a little quieter, or like your beach lined with something other than hotels, head a few miles further south. After passing through still-rural sections of Virginia Beach, you'll come to Sandbridge. Here, at Little Island Park, you won't encounter crowds of people, but you may very well see brown pelicans, laughing gulls, surf scooters, sanderlings, myrtle warblers, piping plovers, boat-tailed grackles, or gray catbirds.

BEACH
www.vbfun.com
800-822-3224

Scooters and skateboards on the boardwalk. Bikes carrying one, two, or four people. Shops selling saltwater taffy, t-shirts saying pretty much anything, temporary tattoos and body piercings, and, of course, pails and buckets for building sandcastles. Mini golf with giant jungle animals and miniature lighthouses. A Ferris wheel overlooking the ocean. Rides through a haunted house, a nightmare mansion, a mirror maze, a fun house, and a time machine. And

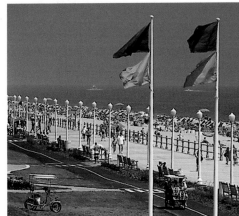

surfers, swimmers, and sunbathers on a wide, sandy beach that extends for miles. Virginia Beach has 'em all.

Virginia Aquarium
www.vmsm.com
757-425-3474

Here you'll find two museums in one: the Atlantic Ocean Pavilion, which houses a series of aquariums, and the Owls Creek Marsh Pavilion about life on the adjacent waterway.

The sharks are in an aquarium that attempts to replicate life in Norfolk Canyon, an unusually deep section of the continental shelf

about sixty miles offshore. In addition to sand tigers and nurse sharks, you can also see jacks and stingrays. The sharks, which only eat when they're hungry, are very well fed (by poles). That way, they're not tempted to munch on the rest of the exhibit.

You can see sea turtles in an environment modeled after that surrounding the Chesapeake Bay Light Tower, which is about seventeen miles off the coast at the point where bay meets ocean. Sea turtles are rarely seen in nature since, unlike their freshwater relatives, they don't like to bask in the sun, though they do have to emerge to breathe. All of the sea turtles here are endangered or threatened.

The Owls Creek Marsh Pavilion has river otters, seahorses, sea roaches, and fiddler crabs.

Virginia Beach Historic Homes
www.virginiabeachhistory.org/houses.html
757-431-4000

Though Virginia Beach doesn't have nearly as many historic homes as Williamsburg, it has a few. The Adam Thoroughgood House was once thought to date back to 1636, which would have made it the oldest brick home in North America. Later research showed it was probably built by one of Thoroughgood's grandsons around 1680. Thoroughgood came to America in 1621 as an indentured servant. He returned to England, married a wealthy woman, and then returned to Virginia, ultimately owning an astounding 5,350 acres, including the site of this house. The house has a seventeenth-century pleasure garden with topiaries, fruit trees, hedges, perennials, and wooden "beasties" to scare away birds and supernatural creatures. Among the furnishings is a rope bed with a wrench to tighten the ropes nightly. (Hence the expression "sleep tight.")

Jump forward a hundred or so years to the Francis Land House. Once surrounded by more than a thousand acres, this plantation, like many of Virginia Beach's old homes, now feels closed in by suburban sprawl. Other historic homes include the 1725 Lynnhaven House and the 1830 Ferry Plantation House. The latter was built on the site of the prison that held Grace Sherwood, a small planter's wife who was accused of witchcraft. In 1706, Sherwood underwent the traditional trial for witches. She was immersed in water. Since she did not drown, she was found guilty.

RICHMOND

There was, wrote John Smith about the site he chose for a 1609 settlement near the falls of the James River, "no place so strong, so pleasant and delightful in Virginia, for which we called it Nonesuch." That settlement, which replaced Williamsburg as the capital in 1780, is now called Richmond. Still, Smith's description remains valid: there is much here that is strong and pleasant and delightful.

Two of Richmond's oldest neighborhoods, Shockoe Slip and Shockoe Bottom, are near downtown and the James River. A trip to the Virginia Historical Society or the Virginia Museum of Fine Arts offers a chance to explore two other lively neighborhoods. Just to the east is the Fan, whose best-known street is Monument Avenue, with its statues of Confederate heroes and Richmond's own tennis legend, Arthur Ashe. West of the Fan is Carytown, with a more condensed but equally eclectic retail mix on Cary Street. Richmond is only an hour's drive west of Williamsburg.

JOHN MARSHALL HOUSE
www.preservationvirginia.org/marshall
804-648-7998

The Constitution may have provided for three branches of government, but it was Chief Justice John Marshall who made the courts a genuinely equal partner with the president and Congress. Marshall established the Supreme Court as the final arbiter of what's constitutional. Said Oliver Wendell Holmes, "If American law were to be represented by a single figure, skeptic and worshipper alike would agree without dispute that the figure could be one alone, and that one, John Marshall." Marshall studied law under George Wythe at the College of William and Mary and served in Congress before becoming, in 1801, chief justice. He held the office until his death in 1835.

His downtown Richmond house, built between 1788 and 1790 and now a property of Preservation Virginia, is an outstanding example of Federal architecture. Nearly half of the furniture and other memorabilia in the house were owned by Marshall or others in his family. Some are associated with his career, for example, his books and writing desk. Others had more personal significance, such as the silver coffeepot and sugar dish Marshall commissioned for his son and daughter-in-law.

St. John's Church
www.historicstjohnschurch.org
804-648-5015

"Is life so dear, or peace so sweet, as to be purchased at the price of chains and slavery?" asked Patrick Henry on March 23, 1775, the fourth day of the second Virginia Convention. Henry and his fellow delegates chose Richmond to meet, putting a safe distance between themselves and the governor in Williamsburg. Richmond was then a small frontier town, and this 1741 church, now the heart of the elegant Church Hill neighborhood, was then the only building that could fit all the delegates. Henry's answer to his own question swayed the delegates to adopt "a posture of Defence": "I know not what course others may take," he said, "but as for me, give me liberty or give me death!"

Virginia Historical Society
www.vahistorical.org
804-358-4901

"All of British North America," noted planter and Richmond founder William Byrd II, "was carved out of Virginia." The significance of Virginia history is crystal clear from a visit to the Historical Society, especially to its main permanent exhibit. "The Story of Virginia" starts sixteen thousand years ago with copper, shell, bone, and stone evidence of the societies that existed here before the Euro-

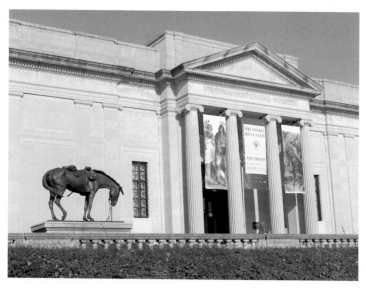

peans. The story proceeds through the initial contacts and conflicts; through the distinctive culture that emerged from English, Indian, African, and later German and Scotch-Irish influences; through Virginia's leading role in the Revolution and the creation of a new nation; and up through the present.

CITIE OF HENRICUS
www.henricus.org
804-748-1613

Founded four years after Jamestown, the Citie of Henricus had more than its share of firsts, among them a charter for the first college in America (it wasn't built, partly because the Indians the colony envisioned as students had little interest in attending) and the first English hospital, Mt. Malady, which had forty beds for eighty patients. Pocahontas lived in the nearby home of the Reverend Whitaker during her courtship with John Rolfe. The site was abandoned after an Indian attack in 1622. Today, the site demonstrates the daily lives of the Indians and English of 1611–1622.

SCOTCHTOWN
www.preservationvirginia.org/scotchtown
804-227-3500

Patrick Henry delivered his most famous speeches in Williamsburg ("If this be treason, make the most of it") and Richmond ("Give me liberty or give me death"), but his home from 1771 to 1775 was at Scotchtown. The house, now a property of Preservation Virginia, was built by the Chiswell family probably in the second third of the eighteenth century. It is architecturally distinct for the undivided attic that runs the full length of the house.

CIVIL WAR BATTLEFIELDS
www.nps.gov/rich
804-226-1981

The battles fought between Williamsburg and Richmond were crucial to the outcome of the Civil War. Robert E. Lee's 1862 offensive, which was given the biblical-sounding name of the Seven Days' Battles, stopped George McClellan's advance toward the capital and prompted Lee to push into Northern Virginia and ultimately

Maryland. Two years later, on nearly the same terrain, it was Ulysses S. Grant who was on the offensive, and Lee's Confederates who were making a desperate stand. Sites preserved from the Seven Days' Battles of 1862 are Malvern Hill, Chickahominy Bluff, Beaver Dam Creek, Gaines' Mill, Glendale, and Drewry's Bluff. From the 1864 campaign, there are Cold Harbor, Garthright House, Fort Harrison, Totopotomoy Creek, and Parker's Battery.

MAGGIE L. WALKER NATIONAL HISTORIC SITE (MAGGIE WALKER HOUSE)
www.nps.gov/mawa
804-771-2017

One of Richmond's best-known entrepreneurs was Maggie Walker, the first woman bank president. Walker's home, now operated by the National Park Service, offers a glimpse at an African-American success story around the turn of the twentieth century. In the library are photos Walker displayed of leaders and artists who inspired (and visited) her, among them Booker T. Washington, W.E.B. DuBois, Langston Hughes, Mary McLeod Bethune, and Paul Dunbar. The surrounding neighborhood, Jackson Ward, was, during its heyday in the 1940s, a dynamic African-American cultural center packed with jazz clubs, theaters, and restaurants.

LEWIS GINTER BOTANICAL GARDEN
www.lewisginter.org
804-262-9887

The Lewis Ginter Botanical Garden blooms year-round with more than fifty acres of gardens. The recently installed rose garden features more than eighteen hundred roses in eighty varieties. Other areas include an extensive perennial garden, an Asian garden, a

wetland garden, and a Victorian garden. In the children's garden, you'll find a wheelchair-accessible tree house. An eleven thousand-square-foot conservatory houses exotic and unusual plants and seasonal displays. One wing features semitropical plants including the garden's orchid collection.

Maymont
www.maymont.org
804-358-7166

To call Maymont a park doesn't do it justice; it's more like an idyllic English estate. The mansion, finished in 1893, still stands, a monument to Victorian opulence. James Henry and Sallie May Dooley loved Tiffany windows, European and Asian porcelain, French tapestry, Oriental rugs, mahogany wood, and swans. The grounds include an arboretum and Italian and Japanese gardens, among others. It seems unbelievable that gardens like these—some formal, some intimate, all spectacular—could be found in a public park. There are also giant aquariums with otters, turtles, and fish; wildlife exhibits that have native Virginian species like bears, foxes, and birds of prey; a children's farm; and an interactive nature center.

Virginia House
www.vahistorical.org/vh/vh_house_main.htm
804-353-4251

Agecroft Hall
www.agecrofthall.com
804-353-4241

Wilton House Museum
www.wiltonhousemuseum.org
804-282-5936

Virginia House.

For the very wealthy of the 1920s, it was fashionable, instead of building your own mansion, to import one. Thus did Virginia House and Agecroft Hall, two grand English manor houses, come to stand side by side in the Windsor Farms neighborhood overlooking the James River just west of downtown Richmond. West of Windsor Farms along Cary Street are many homegrown mansions. There's also Wilton House, a 1753 James River plantation once owned by William Randolph III. Wilton House was originally in Varina, fifteen miles to the east. In 1933, with the house deteriorating and the area around it industrializing, the National Society of the Colonial Dames of America bought Wilton House, and it, too, was packed up and moved to the west.

SCIENCE MUSEUM OF VIRGINIA
www.smv.org
804-864-1400

If you hand a small ball to a rat, what do you expect will happen? If you're thinking the rat will run away, think again. At the Science Museum of Virginia, the most likely scenario is that the rat will drop the ball through a hoop on its small basketball court and then follow the ball through the hoop itself. The shot is known at the museum as a body dunk. Stick around for the rat basketball demonstration and you'll discover operant conditioning. You may also recognize it as positive reinforcement. This is just one of the hundreds of hands-on exhibits here that will teach and surprise you. Right next door is the Children's Museum of Richmond (www.c-mor.org or 804-474-2667), where kids can be artists, inventors . . . or just kids.

VIRGINIA MUSEUM OF FINE ARTS
www.vmfa.state.va.us
804-340-1400

After a major expansion and renovation, the galleries of the Virginia Museum of Fine Arts reopened in May 2010. The collection at the museum spans six thousand years of world art. Don't miss the intricately designed Fabergé eggs, laden with gold and diamonds. These eggs were the Romanovs' favorite Easter gift within the Russian imperial family.

PAMUNKEY MUSEUM
www.baylink.org/Pamunkey
804-843-4792

When most people think of Indians, they think of the West, but the descendants of Powhatan and Pocahontas are still very much alive in Virginia. Some of the Pamunkey, once the most powerful of the tribes in the area, continue to live on a reservation granted them by a 1677 treaty. You can visit by taking a roundabout route from Williamsburg to Richmond. Think of it as another historic triangle, this one formed by Williamsburg, Richmond, and King William County to the north. The reservation's museum covers Virginia Indian history from the Ice Age to the present. Exhibits show how the Indians' hunting, fishing, farming, and trapping techniques evolved. There are also examples of pottery, past and present. The Mattaponi also have a reservation nearby.

CHARLOTTESVILLE AND ENVIRONS

You can often get a sense of how lively a city is from its alternative news weeklies. Charlottesville, remarkably for a small city, has two: *c-ville* and *The Hook*. Each has pages of listings of clubs, music, dance, theater, art, movies, restaurants, classes, and workshops. Charlottesville is about 120 miles west of Williamsburg.

The Downtown Mall, a bricked pedestrian zone, is crammed with restaurants, cafes, galleries, antique stores, gift shops, and bookstores. This area was bustling 250 years ago, and it still is. Most of the stores on the mall are local, not chains. There's also the Virginia Discovery Museum (www.vadm.org or 434-977-1025) for children and an ice skating rink. Right off the mall is Court Square with Charlottesville's original courthouse, a tavern, and about a dozen other buildings from the 1700s and early 1800s.

For more of a student's take on Charlottesville, head to the Corner, just a short walk from the University of Virginia's Rotunda. Here are inexpensive restaurants, coffeehouses, and clubs.

MONTICELLO
www.monticello.org
434-984-9800

Monticello is almost a biography of Jefferson.

"In the very furnishings which Jefferson devised on his own drawing board," said President Franklin Roosevelt, "there speaks ready capacity for detail, and above all, creative genius."

Take the revolving bookstand Jefferson designed, which you can see in his study. It can hold up to five books, each at a different and adjustable angle. No Internet service provider offers quicker access to a wide range of information. Then there's the bed, which Jefferson designed to go in an alcove open to both the study and the bedroom. And the dumbwaiters designed to bring wine from the cellar to the dining room.

Contrary to popular opinion, Jefferson did not invent the copying machine that holds two sheets of paper and two connected pens so that, as he wrote with one, the other followed. He did, however, suggest some improvements to the actual inventor, Charles Willson Peale.

In fact, Jefferson improvised as often as he invented. He designed the great clock in the entrance hall, which is driven by two sets of weights. When he tried to install it at Monticello, he discovered the ropes holding the weights were longer than the height of the hall. So, Jefferson cut a hole in the floor, allowing the weights to continue down to the basement.

The entire house was subject to Jefferson's renovating mind. "Architecture is my delight," Jefferson said, "and putting up, and pulling down, one of my favorite amusements." He ordered his mountaintop leveled in 1768 and first designed a Renaissance villa in stark contrast to the style he was familiar with in Williamsburg. That version of Monticello was mostly done by 1782. After returning from France, Jefferson incorporated many new elements, including the dome, the first on an American building. The new version was completed in 1809.

The gardens, too, were a laboratory for Jefferson. He grew not only food but also plants from around the world. You can also tour Mulberry Row, where some of Jefferson's slaves, including Sally Hemings, once lived. In 1802, the *Richmond Recorder* charged that Hemings was Jefferson's mistress, and the story has haunted Jefferson's reputation since. Genetic tests made in 1998 convinced most historians, including those at Monticello, that Jefferson fathered at least one and maybe all six of Hemings's children.

Beyond Mulberry Row is the graveyard where Jefferson was buried. "I am as happy nowhere else & in no other society," he wrote in 1787, "& all my wishes end, where I hope my days will end, at Monticello."

ASH LAWN-HIGHLAND
www.ashlawnhighland.org
434-293-9539

James Monroe purchased what was then Highland in 1793, mostly because of his friendship with Thomas Jefferson. In fact, Jefferson chose the site, assigned gardeners to start orchards, and had the bricks for the home made at Monticello. In case Monroe needed a reminder of his friend, he could always look out his window and see Monticello. The Blue Ridge Mountains still make a beautiful backdrop for Ash Lawn, though the view of Monticello is now blocked by trees.

UNIVERSITY OF VIRGINIA
www.virginia.edu
434-924-0311

Thomas Jefferson conceived his "academical village" as ten homes for professors attached to two rows of student dorms. At the head of a shared lawn would stand, in significant contrast to the usual chapel, a library.

The Lawn remains the heart of the University of Virginia. Students still vie for rooms on the Lawn, though many undoubtedly prefer a dorm with a bathroom. The Rotunda at the head of the Lawn, which Jefferson modeled after the Pantheon in Rome, no longer holds the university library, but it looks much as it did when it

was completed in 1826. The dome room, which art historian Robert Hughes described as "the round cranium of the university—literally, its brain," still holds some books in cases hidden behind the room's columns—so that they wouldn't interfere with the dinners Jefferson also intended to hold there.

The dome collapsed in 1895 after a misguided effort to stop the spread of a fire by dynamiting the part of the building in flames. Famed architect Stanford White then designed a new and expanded Rotunda, but, as the nation's bicentennial approached, students and alumni raised money to restore Jefferson's original design. It was reopened April 13, 1976, the founder's birthday.

Montpelier
www.montpelier.org
540-672-2728

Montpelier was the lifelong home of James Madison. Madison was raised at Montpelier, lived here with his wife Dolley, returned here after his presidency, and died here in his study surrounded by the books and papers that marked so much of his life's work. It was at Montpelier that Madison researched past democracies and considered new forms of government—work that led his contemporaries to call him "father of the Constitution." The Montpelier estate features the Madison mansion, historic buildings, exhibits, archaeological sites, gardens, forests, and a freedman's cabin and farm.

Surry and Smithfield

For a visit to a more rural Virginia, you can cross the James River to Surry County. You can take the James River Bridge from Newport News, but it's a lot more fun to take the ferry, which leaves from the dock right next to Jamestown Settlement.

Bacon's Castle
www.preservationvirginia.org/baconscastle
757-357-5976

Not only did Nathaniel Bacon not own this house, he probably never set foot in it. But, the house did indeed play a role in Bacon's Rebellion, the 1676 uprising that in some ways foreshadowed the revolution that followed one hundred years later.

The immediate cause of the rebellion was Gov. William Berkeley's failure to adequately protect the white inhabitants of Surry from Indian attacks. Surry was then very much still the frontier. Bacon led a series of unauthorized attacks against Indians, infuriating Berkeley. When Berkeley started raising troops to suppress

the rebels, Bacon attacked Jamestown and burned the town to the ground. Bacon then retreated to Gloucester, but he sent seventy men to his home county of Surry. For four months, they occupied Arthur Allen's house. Allen, a loyal supporter of Berkeley, would have been appalled that his house would become known as Bacon's Castle.

Allen's house is of interest to architectural as well as political historians. Built in 1665, now a property of Preservation Virginia, it's one of the oldest brick houses still standing in North America. The Flemish-style gables and the diagonally set triple chimney give the house a look unlike anything in the area. The house is a rare surviving example of Jacobean architecture in America.

SMITH'S FORT PLANTATION
www.preservationvirginia.org/smithsfort
757-294-3872

John Smith built a fort on this property in 1609, thinking he might have to retreat here if the Spanish or Indians attacked Jamestown. Later, when Pocahontas married John Rolfe (not John Smith), this property again entered the story. Chief Powhatan gave the land to his son-in-law as a dowry.

Pocahontas and John Rolfe never lived on the property: the couple moved to England soon after the wedding. Rolfe did, however, grow tobacco on the property.

Smith's Fort, a property of Preservation Virginia, is an example of a gentry-level mid-eighteenth-century dwelling. The house currently on the property was built between 1751 and 1765 and was home to Jacob Faulcon and his family. Much of the extensive original pine woodwork can still be seen. So can the earthwork of the original fort, which is down a brushy and often muddy path.

Chippokes Plantation State Park
www.dcr.state.va.us/parks/chippoke.htm
757-294-3625

When most people think of Virginia plantations, they envision the grand homes and grounds that still line the north bank of the James River between Richmond and Williamsburg. Those on the southern shore never fared as well, partly because shallower water made their river trade more difficult. Most eventually fell into ruin—with the notable exception of Chippokes.

Chippokes Plantation, taking advantage of its proximity to Jamestown, flourished. Since 1967, Chippokes has been a state park, with a farm museum and a mansion open to the public. Among the farm equipment at the museum is a still, which may have kept the plantation from being destroyed during the Civil War. According to local tradition, Chippokes's owner, Albert Jones, served homemade peach brandy to both Confederate and Union generals. After that, neither side had the heart to burn down the plantation.

Jones built the Italian villa–style mansion in 1854. Behind the mansion are six acres of gardens. If you venture a bit farther, you can follow a trail through the woods to the river or along the edge of the farm to Chippokes Creek.

Smithfield
www.visitSmithfieldIsleofWight.com
757-357-5182
800-365-9939

If you've had enough of John Smith, rest assured that the town was named for Arthur Smith IV, who surveyed this land in 1750. And, if you've had enough of early colonial architecture, Smithfield offers a refreshing jumble of eighteenth- and nineteenth-century houses. Truth be told, Smithfield's Historic Walking Tour features plenty of homes that date back to the seventeenth century, but what stand out are the post–Civil War Victorian homes with their frilly yet elegant turrets and towers and gingerbread trimmings.

Smithfield's most famous product is ham, and, at the Isle of Wight County Museum on Main Street, you can take a look at the world's oldest. Cured in 1902, this ham was part of an order shipped to West Virginia, but, for some reason, it never got there. It was originally eighteen pounds, but it's now a shriveled six.

Just to the east of Smithfield is St. Luke's Church, the oldest Gothic church in America. The brick walls, which are two feet thick, date back to 1632. So do many of the bricks on the floor. The communion table and chairs and the silver baptismal basin are fine examples of seventeenth-century American craftsmanship.

Practical Information

WHERE TO STAY

*C*olonial Williamsburg hotels, located in and around the Historic Area, are convenient to Jamestown and Yorktown as well. For reservations call 1-800-HISTORY (1-800-447-8679) or book online at www.ColonialWilliamsburg.com.

The **Williamsburg Inn** is for many a destination in itself. The hotel offers gourmet dining, an outdoor pool and bathhouse, clay and hard-surface tennis courts, croquet, and lawn bowling. The Inn is also just steps away from the Spa of Colonial Williamsburg and the award-winning Golden Horseshoe Golf Club. John D. Rockefeller Jr., the man behind the restoration of Colonial Williamsburg's Historic Area, played a key role in designing and furnishing the Inn. The hotel is decorated in the Regency style of early nineteenth-century England and has hosted hundreds of VIPs, including presidents and royalty. Guests who seek serene privacy within a resort setting can choose accommodations at the adjacent **Providence Hall**.

For those who want to fully immerse themselves in the eigh-

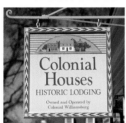

teenth century, the **Colonial Houses–Historic Lodging**, located right in the Historic Area, offers accommodations furnished with authentic period reproductions and antiques accompanied by twenty-first-century amenities.

Across the street from the Historic Area, discover the charm and convenience of the **Williamsburg Lodge.** The Lodge offers the perfect balance of twenty-first-century technology and amenities and old-fashioned southern charm. The Lodge's restaurant features a display kitchen: the chefs move to center stage, providing guests with entertainment

as well as delicious food. The Lodge is just a short stroll from the Spa of Colonial Williamsburg and the Golden Horseshoe Golf Club. Swimming, tennis, croquet, and lawn bowling are available to guests.

The **Williamsburg Woodlands Hotel & Suites**, nestled on the edge of a pine grove, is right next to the visitor center for Colonial

Williamsburg and the Historic Triangle. The moderately priced Williamsburg Woodlands Hotel & Suites is ideal for families. The facility offers bicycle rentals, a children's playground, a horseshoe pit, miniature golf, an outdoor swimming pool (including lap and children's pools), table tennis, and volleyball. The on-site fitness center features cardiovascular and weight-training equipment.

Centrally located only three short walking blocks from the Historic Area, the **Governor's Inn** offers convenience and affordability to families looking to maximize their stay. The Governor's Inn has an outdoor swimming pool, and guests have access to the Williamsburg Woodlands Hotel & Suites fitness center.

The Spa of Colonial Williamsburg offers treatments inspired by five centuries of relaxation and rejuvenation practices. Spa services include massages, body treatments,

baths, professional skin care, and the conservatory salon. The fitness center at the spa includes an aerobics studio, a variety of classes, cardiovascular and weight-training equipment, and personal trainer services and is available to all guests of Colonial Williamsburg Hotels.

WILLIAMSBURG AREA HOTELS

AMERICA'S BEST VALUE INN
HISTORIC WILLIAMSBURG
119 Bypass Road
757-253-1663
www.abviwilliamsburg.com

BEST WESTERN HISTORIC AREA
201 Bypass Road
757-220-0880
www.williamsburgvacations.com

CLARION HOTEL HISTORIC
DISTRICT
351 York Street
757-229-4100
www.clarionwilliamsburg.com

COLONIAL HOUSES–HISTORIC
LODGING
An official Colonial Williamsburg Hotel
136 E. Francis Street
800-447-8679
www.colonialwilliamsburg.com

COURTYARD BY MARRIOTT
WILLIAMSBURG
470 McLaws Circle
757-221-0700
www.courtyardwilliamsburg.com

CROWNE PLAZA WILLIAMSBURG
AT FT. MAGRUDER
6945 Pocahontas Trail
757-220-2250
www.cpwilliamsburghotel.com

GOVERNOR'S INN
An official Colonial Williamsburg Hotel
506 N. Henry Street
800-447-8679
www.colonialwilliamsburg.com

GREAT WOLF LODGE
WILLIAMSBURG
549 E. Rochambeau Drive
757-229-9700
www.greatwolflodge.com

KINGSMILL RESORT & SPA
1010 Kingsmill Road
757-253-3948
www.kingsmill.com

LA QUINTA INNS & SUITES
814 Capitol Landing Road
757-229-0200
www.6442.lq.com

LEXINGTON GEORGE WASHINGTON
INN & CONFERENCE CENTER
500 Merrimac Trail
757-220-1410
www.lgwinn.com

MARRIOTT WILLIAMSBURG HOTEL
50 Kingsmill Road
757-220-2500
www.williamsburgmarriott.com

PATRIOT INN AND SUITES
1420 Richmond Road
757-229-2981
www.patriotinnandsuites.com

PINEAPPLE INN AND HOUSING
CENTER
5437 Richmond Road
757-259-9670
www.pineapplehousing.com

PROVIDENCE HALL GUESTHOUSES
An official Colonial Williamsburg Hotel
305 S. England Street
800-447-8679
www.colonialwilliamsburg.com

QUALITY SUITES WILLIAMSBURG
1406 Richmond Road
757-220-9304
www.choicehotels.com/hotel/va837

RESIDENCE INN BY MARRIOTT
WILLIAMSBURG
1648 Richmond Road
757-941-2000
www.marriott.com/phfrw

SPRINGHILL SUITES BY MARRIOTT
1644 Richmond Road
757-941-3000
www.marriott.com/phfsh

WEDMORE PLACE AT THE
 WILLIAMSBURG WINERY
5810 Wessex Hundred
757-941-0317
www.wedmoreplace.com

WILLIAMSBURG HOSPITALITY
 HOUSE
415 Richmond Road
757-229-4020
www.williamsburghosphouse.com

WILLIAMSBURG INN
An official Colonial Williamsburg Hotel
136 E. Francis Street
757-220-7610
www.colonialwilliamsburg.com

WILLIAMSBURG LODGE
An official Colonial Williamsburg Hotel
310 S. England Street
800-447-8679
www.colonialwilliamsburg.com

WILLIAMSBURG WOODLANDS
 HOTEL & SUITES
An official Colonial Williamsburg Hotel
105 Visitor Center Drive
800-447-8679
www.colonialwilliamsburg.com

YORKTOWN MOTOR LODGE
8829 George Washington
 Memorial Highway
757-898-5451
www.yorktownmotorlodge.com

Williamsburg Area
Bed and Breakfasts

Autumn Leaves
Bed & Breakfast
520 Jamestown Road
757-253-8977
www.autumnleavesbandb.com

Cedars of Williamsburg
Bed & Breakfast
616 Jamestown Road
757-229-3591
www.cedarsofwilliamsburg.com

Colonial Capital Bed &
Breakfast
501 Richmond Road
757-229-0233
www.ccbb.com

The Fife & Drum Inn
441 Prince George Street
757-345-1776
www.fifeanddruminn.com

Governor's Trace
Bed & Breakfast
303 Capitol Landing Road
757-229-7552

Magnolia Manor
Bed & Breakfast
700 Richmond Road
757-220-9600
www.magnoliamanorwmbg.com

Newport House
Bed & Breakfast
710 S. Henry Street
757-229-1775
www.newporthousebb.com

Simpson House Cottage
10 Bayberry Lane
757-220-3575

War Hill Inn Bed & Breakfast
4560 Longhill Road
757-565-0248
www.warhillinn.com

Williamsburg Sampler
Bed & Breakfast
922 Jamestown Road
757-253-0398
www.williamsburgsampler.com

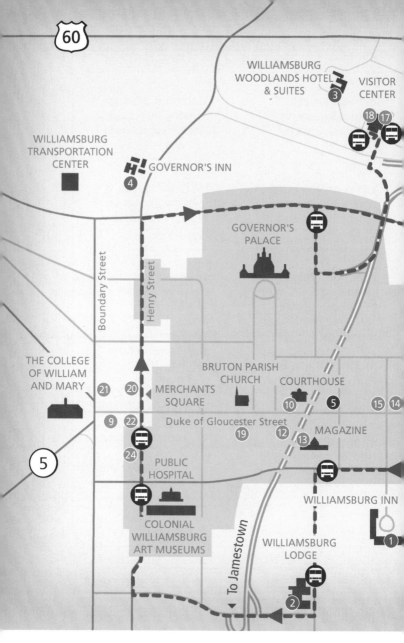

HOTELS

1. Williamsburg Inn
2. Williamsburg Lodge
3. Williamsburg Woodlands Hotel & Suites
4. Governor's Inn

HISTORIC DINING TAVERNS

5. Chowning's Tavern
6. King's Arms Tavern
7. Shields Tavern
8. Christiana Campbell's Tavern

SHOPS

9. Kimball Theatre
10. Mary Dickinson Store
11. The Golden Ball
12. John Greenhow Store
13. Market Square (Seasonal)
14. Post Office
15. Prentis Store
16. Tarpley's Store
17. Williamsburg Booksellers
18. Williamsburg Revolutions

Colonial Williamsburg's Historic Area

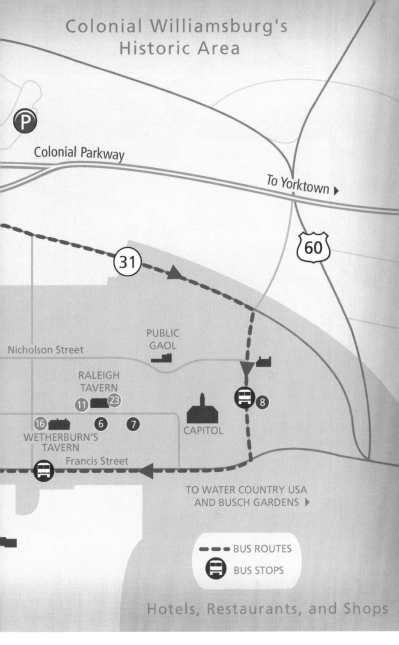

- - - BUS ROUTES

🚌 BUS STOPS

Hotels, Restaurants, and Shops

19 Colonial Garden and Nursery (seasonal)
20 Everything Williamsburg
21 Williamsburg At Home
22 Williamsburg Craft House
23 Raleigh Tavern Bakery
24 Williamsburg Celebrations

239

WHERE TO EAT

COLONIAL WILLIAMSBURG'S HISTORIC AREA

At Colonial Williamsburg's historic dining taverns, you can get a taste of the ambience and food that George Washington and others enjoyed in the colonial capital. The taverns are all located within the Historic Area.

Washington, by the way, went to Christiana Campbell's Tavern twenty-one times between March 2 and April 9 of 1772. Sometimes he was joined by Martha Washington, her two children, and friends. Locals and visitors alike flocked to Williamsburg's taverns, especially during "Publick Times," when the General Court was in session.

KING'S ARMS TAVERN

The King's Arms Tavern served an elite crowd. With customers like George Washington, Thomas Nelson, and Baron von Steuben, it's easy to see why, when revolution broke out, owner Jane Vobe abandoned the royal name and started calling it simply "Mrs. Vobe's" and later the "Eagle Tavern."

The King's Arms Tavern serves lunch and dinner. Breakfast is served seasonally Friday through Sunday. You can check the opening schedule and make reservations at the Visitor Center Dining and Lodging Reservations Desk or by calling 1-800-TAVERNS or (757) 229-2141.

CHRISTIANA CAMPBELL'S TAVERN

Christiana Campbell's Tavern was George Washington's favorite for seafood. Today, it's known as Colonial Williamsburg's premier seafood tavern and serves up regional delights. Guests can also expect warm hospitality and may even be visited by Mrs. Campbell or her daughter Molly during the evening.

Christiana Campbell's Tavern serves lunch and dinner. You can check the opening schedule and make reservations at the Visitor Center Dining and Lodging Reservations Desk or by calling 1-800-TAVERNS or (757) 229-2141.

Chowning's Tavern

During the day, Chowning's Tavern offers quick meals such as stew and sandwiches. You can sit in the grape arbor or inside the tavern. After 5 p.m., Chowning's turns into an alehouse serving light fare, local ales and wines, rums, and Colonial Williamsburg's own draft root beer and ginger ale. The nighttime program includes balladeers who lead period sing-alongs and costumed servers who teach you popular card and board games of the era. Chowning's is faring better today than it did for Josiah Chowning, who, like many others, found that the hotel and restaurant business is difficult. In 1766, after eighteen months of running the tavern, he sold it.

Chowning's Tavern does not take reservations.

Shields Tavern

In the early 1740s, James Shields assumed proprietorship of the tavern that his father-in-law had operated several decades earlier. He operated the tavern until his death in 1750. In 1751, Daniel Fisher took it over.

Tavern guests today dine on southern comfort foods inspired by "colonial receipts."

You can check the opening schedule and make reservations at

the Visitor Center Dining and Lodging Reservations Desk or by calling 1-800-TAVERNS or (757) 229-2141.

Raleigh Tavern Bakery

For those who'd like take-out refreshments in the Historic Area,
perhaps to watch the bustle on Duke of Gloucester Street or to enjoy
the quiet of a nearby garden, the Raleigh Tavern Bakery has sandwiches, beverages, and baked goods.

Merchants Square

Adjacent to the Historic Area, in Merchants Square, you can
find a range of eateries from award-winning restaurants to a quick
slice of pizza. **Aromas Coffee and Café** (757-221-6676) offers full
breakfasts, lunches, light dinners, coffees, teas, and fruit smoothies.
Berret's Restaurant & Taphouse Grill (757-253-1847) serves
regional seafood favorites, including clams, oysters, crabs, chow-
ders, sandwiches, and finfish. The wine menu highlights Virginia
wines and beers. **Blue Talon Bistro** presents classic comfort food
(757-476-2583) in a relaxed neighborhood eatery. **Fat Canary**
(757-229-3333) is acclaimed for its unique American cuisine served
in an intimate and high-energy atmosphere. **Seasons Restaurant**

(757-259-0018) offers steaks, seafood, pasta, burgers, baby back ribs, and salads as well as a weekend brunch and children's menu. **Stephanos Pizza & Subs** (757-476-8999) has New York–style pizza (by the slice if you want) and oven-baked sandwiches.

Trellis Restaurant (757-229-8610) serves contemporary American cuisine in an elegant modern setting.

Specialty food shops include **Baskin-Robbins** (757-229-6385), with a variety of ice creams, milk shakes, malts, sundaes, and frozen yogurts. The **Cheese Shop** (757-220-1324) has more than two hundred imported and domestic cheeses, great wines, freshly baked breads, specialty foods, and its renowned sandwiches. **Pizza on the Square** (757-565-8588), the concession stand at the Kimball Theatre, offers snacks and beverages. **Wythe Candy & Gourmet Shop** (757-229-4406) has handcrafted candies, nuts, and treats.

OTHER COLONIAL WILLIAMSBURG EATERIES

Colonial Williamsburg offers a range of dining experiences outside the Historic Area.

Enjoy elegant dining at the Williamsburg Inn's **Regency Room,** which has hosted kings and queens as well as presidents. Choose your meal from an award-winning menu and wine list, with dancing on Friday and Saturday nights. The Inn's **Restoration Bar** and **Terrace Room** offer light fare and afternoon tea.

The dining room at the Williamsburg Lodge features an open finishing kitchen and traditional regional specialties. Guests enjoy the main dining room, and small groups may arrange to dine in one of three private rooms—ideal for conferees looking to continue business discussions over a meal.

The variety of salads, sandwiches, and oven-baked pizza will make you shout **Huzzah!** when you visit this family-friendly restaurant adjacent to the Visitor Center. Inside WILLIAMSBURG Booksellers at the Colonial Williamsburg Visitor Center, **Commonweath Coffee and Tea** offers gourmet coffees and teas, lattes, soft drinks, and pastries. **The Golden Horseshoe Gold Course Clubhouse Grill**

offers a sweeping view of the golf course along with savory salads and sandwiches. **The Green Course Clubhouse Grill** offers a more limited menu. While touring the DeWitt Wallace Decorative Arts Museum and the Abby Aldrich Rockefeller Folk Art Museum, take a break for the fare available at the **Museum Café.**

For reservations at Colonial Williamsburg's restaurants or taverns, stop at the Visitor Center Dining and Lodging Reservations Desk or call 1-800-TAVERNS or (757) 229-2141. Menus are subject to change.

For current hours of operation for Colonial Williamsburg and Merchants Square dining establishments, check Colonial Williamsburg's monthly dining and shopping guide.

WILLIAMSBURG AREA RESTAURANTS
$ *(under $7)*, $$ *($7–15)*, $$$ *($15–21)*, $$$$ *(over $21)*
Seasonal hours may apply. Holiday closings vary.

415 GRILL
415 Richmond Road
American, Regional, Seafood
Open daily
Lunch $$
Dinner $$
757-229-4020

ABERDEEN BARN
1601 Richmond Road
Steakhouse, Seafood, American
Open daily
Dinner $$$
757-229-6661

ALIZE BISTRO
601 Prince George Street
American, Seafood, Steakhouse
Open daily
Lunch $$
Dinner $$$$
757-258-8882

BACKFIN SEAFOOD RESTAURANT
3701 Strawberry Plains Road
Seafood
Closed Sundays
Lunch $
Dinner $$
757-565-5430

BERRET'S RESTAURANT
199 S. Boundary Street
Seafood
Open daily
Lunch $
Dinner $$$$
757-253-1847

BLACK ANGUS GRILL
1433 Richmond Road
Steakhouse, Seafood, Regional
Open daily
Dinner $$$
757-229-6823

BLUE TALON BISTRO
420 Prince George Street
French, American, Regional
Open daily
Lunch $$
Dinner $$$
757-476-2583

BONEFISH GRILL
5212 Monticello Avenue
Seafood
Open daily
Dinner $$$
757-229-3474

BRAY BISTRO
1010 Kingsmill Road
American, Seafood, Fine Dining
Open daily
Breakfast $$
Lunch $$
Dinner $$$$
757-259-2900

CAPITOL PANCAKE HOUSE
802 Capitol Landing Road
Breakfast, American
Open daily
Breakfast $
Lunch $
757-564-1238

CASA MAYA
1660 Richmond Road
Mexican
Open daily
Lunch $
Dinner $$
757-259-2470

CENTER STREET GRILL
5101 Center Street
American
Open daily
Lunch $$
Dinner $$$
757-220-4600

CHILI'S
1652 Richmond Road
American, Regional
Open daily
Lunch $$
Dinner $$
757-229-9865

CHOWNING'S TAVERN
416 E. Duke of Gloucester Street
American
Open daily
Seasonal closings
Lunch $
Dinner $$
757-229-1000

CHRISTIANA CAMPBELL'S TAVERN
101 S. Waller Street
Seafood, American
Opening schedule varies
Seasonal closings
Lunch $$
Dinner $$$$
757-229-1000

CITIES GRILLE
4511 John Tyler Highway
Regional, American
Open daily
Lunch $$
Dinner $$$
757-564-3955

COLONIAL HERITAGE CLUB
6500 Arthur Hills Drive
American, Regional
Open daily
Lunch $$
Dinner $$$
757-240-1498

COLONIAL PANCAKE HOUSE
100 Page Street
Breakfast, American
Open daily
Breakfast $
Lunch $
757-253-5852

COPPER SCROLL
500 Merrimac Trail
American
Open daily
Lunch $
Dinner $$
757-220-1410

CRACKER BARREL
200 Bypass Road
American, Breakfast
Open daily
Breakfast $
Lunch $
Dinner $
757-220-3384

DORALDO'S RISTORANTE ITALIANO
1915 Pocahontas Trail
Italian, Pizza
Open Daily
Lunch $$
Dinner $$$
757-220-0795

DUDLEY'S FARMHOUSE GRILLE
7816 Richmond Road
American
Open Daily
Lunch $$
Dinner $$$
757-566-1157

EAGLES STEAKHOUSE
1010 Kingsmill Road
Steakhouse, Regional
Open daily
Breakfast $$
Lunch $$
Dinner $$$$
757-259-2900

FIRESIDE CHOP HOUSE
1995 Richmond Road
Steakhouse, American, Seafood
Open daily
Lunch $$
Dinner $$$
757-229-3310

FOOD FOR THOUGHT
1647 Richmond Road
American
Open Daily
Lunch $
Dinner $$
757-645-4665

GABRIEL ARCHER TAVERN
5800 Wessex Hundred
Regional
Open daily for lunch; dinner is
   available from April through
   October Thursday–Saturday
Lunch $$
Dinner $$$
757-229-0999

GAZEBO HOUSE OF PANCAKES
409 Bypass Road
Breakfast, American
Open daily
Breakfast $
Lunch $
757-220-0883

GIUSEPPE'S ITALIAN CAFÉ
5525 Olde Towne Road
Italian, Mediterranean
Open daily
Lunch $
Dinner $$
757-565-1977

GOLDEN CORRAL
218 Bypass Road
American
Open daily
Breakfast $$
Lunch $$
Dinner $$
757-229-3785

GOLDEN HORSESHOE GOLD
   COURSE CLUBHOUSE GRILL
401 S. England Street
American
Open daily
Seasonal closings
Lunch $
Dinner $$
757-229-1000

GOLDEN HORSESHOE GREEN
   COURSE CLUBHOUSE GRILL
520 S. England Street
American
Open daily
Seasonal closings
Lunch $
Dinner $$
757-229-1000

GREAT WOLF LODGE
549 E. Rochambeau Drive
American
Open daily
Breakfast $
Lunch $
Dinner $$$
757-229-9700

GREEN LEAFE NEW TOWN
4345 New Town Avenue
American
Open daily
Lunch $
Dinner $$
757-476-2233

HOG WILD SMOKEHOUSE
8864 Richmond Road
American
Open daily
Lunch $
Dinner $$
757-741-2575

HOOTERS OF WILLIAMSBURG
112 Bypass Road
American, Seafood
Open daily
Lunch $$
Dinner $$
757-221-9570

HUZZAH!
113 Visitor Center Drive
American, Pizza, Regional
Open daily
Seasonal closings
Lunch $$
Dinner $$
757-565-8800

JEFFERSON RESTAURANT
1453 Richmond Road
American, Italian, Seafood
Open daily
Dinner $$$
757-229-2296

J. M. RANDALLS
4854-16 Longhill Road
American, Regional
Open daily
Breakfast $
Lunch $
Dinner $$
757-259-0406

KING'S ARMS TAVERN
409 E. Duke of Gloucester Street
American, Steakhouse, Regional
Opening schedule varies
Seasonal closings
Lunch $$
Dinner $$$$
757-229-1000

KINGSMILL RESORT
1010 Kingsmill Road
American, Steakhouse, Pizza
Open daily
Breakfast $$
Lunch $$
Dinner $$$
757-253-3913

KYOTO JAPANESE STEAK & SEAFOOD HOUSE
1621 Richmond Road
Japanese, Seafood, Steakhouse
Open daily
Dinner $$
757-220-8888

LE YACA
1915 Pocahontas Trail, Suite C-10
French, Fine Dining
Closed Sundays and
  Saturday lunch
Lunch $$
Dinner $$$$
757-220-3616

LITTLE MAURIZIO'S ITALIAN AMERICAN GRILL
801-E Merrimac Trail
Italian, Pizza, Deli
Open daily
Lunch $
Dinner $$
757-258-5300

LONG JOHN SILVER'S
736 Merrimac Trail
Seafood, American
Open daily
Lunch $
Dinner $
757-229-1924

MAMA STEVE'S HOUSE OF PANCAKES
1509 Richmond Road
Breakfast, American
Open daily
Breakfast $
Lunch $
757-229-7613

MARINA DECK
1010 Kingsmill Road
American, Fine Dining
Open daily
Lunch $$$
Dinner $$$
757-259-2900

MAURIZIO'S ITALIAN
    RESTAURANT
264-E McLaws Circle
Italian
Open daily
Lunch $
Dinner $$
757-229-0337

NATIONAL PANCAKE HOUSE
7105 Pocahontas Trail
Breakfast, American
Open daily
Breakfast $
Lunch $
757-220-9433

NATIONAL PANCAKE HOUSE II
1605 Richmond Road
Breakfast
Open daily
Breakfast $
757-220-5542

NAWAB INDIAN CUISINE
204 Monticello Avenue
Indian
Open daily
Lunch $$
Dinner $$
757-565-3200

NEW YORK DELI & PIZZA
    RESTAURANT
6546 Richmond Road
Pizza, American
Open daily
Lunch $
Dinner $$
757-564-9258

NICK'S RIVERWALK RESTAURANT
323 Water Street
Yorktown
American
Open daily

Lunch $$
Dinner $$$$
757-875-1525

OLD MILL PANCAKE HOUSE
2005 Richmond Road
Breakfast, American
Open daily
Breakfast $
Lunch $
757-229-3613

OPUS 9 STEAKHOUSE
5143 Main Street
Steakhouse
Open daily
Lunch $$
Dinner $$$
757-645-4779

OUTBACK STEAKHOUSE
3026 Richmond Road
Steakhouse
Open daily
Dinner $$$
757-229-8648

PEKING & MONGOLIAN GRILL
    RESTAURANT
120-J Waller Mill Road
Chinese, Japanese, American
Open daily
Lunch $
Dinner $
757-229-2288

POLO CLUB RESTAURANT
1303 Jamestown Road
American, Seafood
Open daily
Lunch $
Dinner $$
757-220-1122

RED HOT & BLUE
1624 Richmond Road
American
Open daily
Lunch $
Dinner $$
757-259-1670

REGATTAS
1010 Kingsmill Road
American, Fine Dining, Pizza
Open daily
Lunch $$
Dinner $$
757-259-2900

SAL'S BY VICTOR
1242 Richmond Road
Italian, Pizza, Seafood
Open daily
Lunch $
Dinner $$
757-220-2641

SAL'S RISTORANTE ITALIANO
835 Capitol Landing Road
Italian, Pizza
Open daily
Lunch $
Dinner $$
757-221-0443

SEAFARE OF WILLIAMSBURG
1632 Richmond Road
Seafood, Steakhouse
Open daily
Dinner $$$
757-229-0099

SEASONS RESTAURANT
110 S. Henry Street
American
Open daily
Lunch $$
Dinner $$$
757-259-0018

SECOND STREET RESTAURANT
140 Second Street
American
Open daily
Lunch $$
Dinner $$
757-220-2286

**SHACKLEFORD'S II
RESTAURANT & RAW BAR**
4640-7 Monticello Avenue
American, Seafood, Regional
Open daily
Dinner $$
757-258-5559

SHIELDS TAVERN
422 E. Duke of Gloucester Street
American, Regional
Open daily
Seasonal closings
Breakfast $
Lunch $
Dinner $$
757-229-1000

STEPHANOS PIZZA & SUBS
110 S. Henry Street
Pizza, American
Open daily
Lunch $
Dinner $$
757-476-8999

TAVERN AT 1776
725 Bypass Road
American, Regional, Seafood
Open daily
Breakfast $
Dinner $$
757-941-1157

TRELLIS
403 W. Duke of Gloucester Street
American, Regional
Open daily
Lunch $$
Dinner $$$$
757-229-8610

WHALING COMPANY
494 McLaws Circle
Seafood, Steakhouse
Open daily
Dinner $$$
757-229-0275

**WILLIAMSBURG INN
REGENCY ROOM**
300 E. Francis Street
Fine Dining, Regional, American
Open daily
Breakfast $$
Lunch $$
Dinner $$$$
757-229-1000

SHOPPING

*W*illiamsburg was a center not only of politics in the eighteenth century but also of shopping and style. It still is.

In Colonial Williamsburg's Historic Area, you can find everything from three-cornered hats to sterling silver hollowware, from medicinal herbs to smoked hams. Adjacent to the Historic Area is Merchants Square, a retail village of remarkable eighteenth century–style buildings. Just a short drive from the Historic Area are outlet malls with national brand-name stores. And, in Yorktown, Riverwalk Landing has revitalized the waterfront with an eclectic mix of shops and a dock for tall ships. For those who prefer to shop online, simply visit www.WilliamsburgMarketplace.com for a selection of WILLIAMSBURG products that support the Colonial Williamsburg Foundation's award-winning educational programs.

COLONIAL WILLIAMSBURG'S HISTORIC AREA

Prentis Store is the oldest surviving commercial structure in Williamsburg. The building played a small part in the Revolution. In 1774, the year after the Boston Tea Party, Virginians threw two chests of tea into the York River from a ship tied up at Yorktown. The tea was on its way to Prentis and Company. The store today offers one-of-a-kind Historic Trades products, including leather goods, men's clothing, iron hardware, and reproduction pottery. All are handmade by tradespeople in the Historic Area using eighteenth-century tools and methods. **Tarpley's Store**, opened in 1755 by merchant James Tarpley, is today geared toward children. Many handcrafted toys and games are available as well as candies, period clothing, and hats. **The Golden Ball** sells many of the same pieces advertised by jeweler James Craig in the eighteenth century, including sterling silver hollowware pieces made by the silversmith next door. At the **John Greenhow Store,** you can still find items Greenhow sold in the eighteenth century, including willow baskets, fine imported porcelain, floorcloths, fabrics, cooper's items, tinware, and craftsmen's tools. The **Mary Dickinson Store** is the place for

a beribboned hat, silver and gold jewelry, and embroidered stockings like those milliner Mary Dickinson sold. At the **Post Office**, you can mail real letters and postcards. They are hand-canceled with a replica of the eighteenth-century Williamsburg postmark. The store also sells copies of the *Virginia Gazette* from 1774, prints, stationery, pens, and ink. The **Raleigh Tavern Bakery** sells food and food-related gifts, along with fresh cookies, cakes, and breads made from eighteenth-century recipes. In season, don't miss the open-air **Colonial Nursery**, with herbs, flowers, seasonal greens, and wreaths along with colonial-style flowerpots, bird bottles, and watering cans, and **Market Square**, where you can buy toys, hats, pottery, baskets, and refreshments.

OTHER COLONIAL WILLIAMSBURG SHOPS

Some excellent shops are just outside the Historic Area, hidden away in Colonial Williamsburg's hotels and museums. The **Colonial Williamsburg Museums Store** has gifts, reproductions, collectibles, books, and recordings reflecting the museums' extensive collections of folk art and fine decorative arts. The **Regency Shop at the Williamsburg Inn** offers exquisite gifts, including fragrances and collectibles. The **Williamsburg Lodge Gift Shop** features gifts with a Virginia theme, and the **Williamsburg Woodlands Hotel & Suites Gift Shop** has a collection of souvenirs. The **Golden Horseshoe Gold and Green Course Pro Shops** carry a large selection of clothes and gifts for golfers. At the Colonial Williamsburg Visitor Center, **WILLIAMSBURG Booksellers** has an extensive collection of history books, videos, CDs, and tapes, especially on the colonial and Revolutionary periods. Inside the bookstore, **Commonwealth Coffee and Tea** offers gourmet coffees and teas, lattes, cappuccino, soft drinks, and pastries. **WILLIAMSBURG Revolutions** sells gifts, toys, and a large selection of souvenirs.

MERCHANTS SQUARE

For gifts and accessories, **G. Bates Ltd**. (757-229-5400) has what you need for your home and garden. The **Campus Shop**

(757-229-4301) carries licensed College of William and Mary merchandise, clothing, and gifts. **Everything WILLIAMSBURG** (757-565-8476) has a broad selection of Colonial Williamsburg logo products from T-shirts to tavernware. **Gallery on Merchants Square** (757-565-8476) offers paintings and sculpture by established artists. **Quilts Unlimited** (757-253-8700) offers more than just quilts—you'll also find colonial clothing, home accessories, and Virginia gifts. **Shirley Pewter Shop** (757-229-5356) has an extensive selection of pewter, including Shirley pewter handcrafted in Williamsburg. At **the Silver Vault Ltd.** (757-220-3777), you can find sterling jewelry, silver hollowware and frames, sterling and silver-plated baby gifts, and tabletop accessories. The **Nancy Thomas Gallery** (757-259-1938) has unique art from folk artist Nancy Thomas. **WILLIAMSBURG Celebrations** (757-565-8642) offers a full assortment of official WILLIAMSBURG holiday decorations, permanent floral arrangements, garden accessories, and classic collectibles. At **WILLIAMSBURG Craft House** (757-220-7747), you'll find a variety of WILLIAMSBURG gifts and tabletop products inspired by the eighteenth century, including dinnerware, flatware, glassware, silver and pewter accents, fine ceramic giftware, paper products, and jewelry—not to mention world-class engravers. **WILLIAMSBURG At Home** (757-220-7749) features inspired home furnishings and accessories from authentic reproductions to creative interpretations of Colonial Williamsburg antiques. Products include furniture, bedding, rugs, lighting, prints, fabrics, bath accessories, and wallpapers.

Merchants Square also offers a wide selection of clothing shops for men, women, and children. **Bella Lingerie and Loungewear** (757-220-8440) has the finest lingerie from around the world. **Binns** (757-229-3391) has women's sportswear, dresses, apparel for special occasions, shoes, accessories, and cosmetics and a luxury gift boutique. **Birkenstock Footprints** (757-229-6999) sells shoes designed to fit the shape of the foot. **R. Bryant Ltd.** (757-253-0055) offers traditional menswear. **The Carousel Children's Clothier** (757-229-1710) offers children's clothing and accessories. **Chico's** (757-564-7448) carries everything from everyday clothing to elegant

eveningwear. **Classic Cravats** (757-229-0055) has fine men's neckwear and accessories. **Ocean Palm** (757-229-3961) offers fashionable resort wear for women and children. **Scotland House Ltd.** (757-229-7800) has fine apparel and gifts from the British Isles. **Talbots** (757-253-6532) offers classic apparel for misses and petites. **Closet Envy** (757-220-0456) offers exceptional women's clothing and accessories.

Specialty shops include the **Christmas Shop** (757-229-2514), featuring Williamsburg-themed ornaments and holiday decorations. **King's Treasure** (757-229-2082) offers home decor, apparel, and gifts. **J. Fenton Gallery** (757-221-8200), an artisan shop, has wood and glass designs, kaleidoscopes, jewelry, handbags, and clothing. At **the Peanut Shop** (757-229-3908), you'll find hand-cooked home-style Virginia peanuts, hams, and other delicacies. **The Precious Gem** (757-220-1115) has custom-designed jewelry with diamond, sapphire, ruby, and solid gold. **The Toymaker of Williamsburg** (757-229-5660) has toy soldiers, games, dolls, and puzzles. **Williams-Sonoma** (757-220-0450) is the destination for home cooks, with an exceptional selection of cookware, tools, linens, cookbooks, distinctive foods, and ingredients. **Mrs. Bones Bowtique** (757-564-0500) has fabulous gifts for pet lovers. **The College of William and Mary Bookstore and Café** (757-253-4900), run by Barnes and Noble, features books, music CDs, DVDs, a children's department, William and Mary clothing and gifts, and a café.

WILLIAMSBURG AREA SHOPPING

BELK
Windsormeade Marketplace
4900-3 Monticello Avenue
757-220-9143
Department store

BELLA LINGERIE AND
    LOUNGEWEAR
Merchants Square
427 Duke of Gloucester Street
757-220-8440
Women's lingerie

CAMPUS SHOP
Merchants Square
425 Prince George Street
757-229-4301
William and Mary merchandise
    and souvenirs

CAROUSEL CHILDREN'S
    CLOTHIER
Merchants Square
420 Duke of Gloucester Street
757-229-1710
Children's clothing

CHRISTMAS MOUSE
1991 Richmond Road
757-221-0357
Christmas decorations and
    collectibles

CHRISTMAS SHOP
Merchants Square
Duke of Gloucester Street
757-229-2514
Williamsburg's oldest Christmas
    store

CLOSET ENVY
Merchants Square
409 Duke of Gloucester Street
757-220-0456
Women's apparel and accessories

DOLLS OF DIANE
2850 Sandy Bay Road, Suite 101
757-345-0029
Novelty gifts and doll exhibits

FLOWER CUPBOARD
205 N. Boundary Street
757-220-0057
Florist and decorations

GARDEN FLAGS
Williamsburg Shopping Center
230 Monticello Avenue
757-293-3524
Garden and house flags

GENUINE SMITHFIELD HAM
    SHOPPE OF WILLIAMSBURG
Merchants Square
421 Prince George Street
757-258-8604
Smithfield and Virginia specialty
    foods

KILWINS
High Street
1430 High Street, Suite 801
757-345-2290
Candy and nuts

KING'S TREASURE
Merchants Square
424 Duke of Gloucester Street
757-229-2082
Souvenirs

LAMPLIGHTER SHOPPE
1322 Jamestown Road
757-565-4676
Reproduction lighting

MASTER CRAFTSMEN SHOP
221 N. Boundary Street
757-253-2993
Silver and pewter ware

MERCHANTS SQUARE
Duke of Gloucester Street
757-220-7751
Exceptional shopping and dining

NAUTICAL DOG
New Town
5104 Main Street
757-220-2001
Gift items

NEW TOWN
4801 Courthouse Street,
Suite 203
757-565-6200
Shopping, restaurants,
entertainment

PAISLEY
New Town
5138 Main Street
757-229-5624
Gifts and accessories

PEANUT SHOP OF
WILLIAMSBURG
Merchants Square
414 Prince George Street
757-229-3908
Virginia peanuts and gifts

PRECIOUS GEM
Merchants Square
423 Duke of Gloucester Street
757-220-1115
Fine jewelry

PRIME OUTLETS OF
WILLIAMSBURG
5715-62A Richmond Road
757-565-0702
120 designer outlets

RIVERWALK LANDING
425 Water Street
Yorktown
757-890-3300
Shops and galleries on the
York River

SCOTLAND HOUSE LTD.
Merchants Square
430 Duke of Gloucester Street
757-229-7800
Gifts and apparel from Scotland,
Ireland, and England

SHIRLEY PEWTER SHOP
Merchants Square
1209 Jamestown Road
757-229-5356
Fine quality pewter reproductions

SHOPS AT HIGH STREET
1424 Richmond Road
757-258-5600
Retail shopping area

TU TIENDA AND GIFTS
122 Waller Mill Road, Suite I
757-220-2255
Spanish food and gifts

VANITY FAIR OUTLET
Williamsburg Outlet Mall
6401 Richmond Road, Suite 30
757-220-9984
Men's, women's, and children's
apparel

WALGREENS
1309 Richmond Road
757-229-0962
Drugstore

WALLACE'S TRADING POST
1851 Richmond Road
757-564-6101
Gifts

WILLIAMSBURG ANTIQUE MALL
500 Lightfoot Road
757-564-3422
Over three hundred antique
dealers

WILLIAMSBURG GENERAL STORE
1656 Richmond Road
757-564-5800
Gifts and Häagen-Dazs ice cream
shop

WILLIAMSBURG OUTLET MALL
6401 Richmond Road
757-565-3378
Outlet shopping

YANKEE CANDLE COMPANY
2200 Richmond Road
757-258-1002
Candles, gifts, and holiday shops

Art

BEAD HAVEN
Village Shops at Kingsmill
1915 Pocahontas Trail, Suite E4
757-253-2323
Full-service bead store

BLACK DOG GALLERY
114 Ballard Street
Yorktown
757-898-1700
Antique prints, maps, and
distinctive framing

GALLERY LOUISE CHARTRAND
8655 Merry Oaks Lane
757-250-3234
Paintings and other fine objects

GALLERY AT YORK HALL
301 Main Street
Yorktown
757-890-4490
Fine art and crafts by local
artists

J. FENTON GALLERY
Merchants Square
110 S. Henry Street
757-221-8200
Fine American crafts featuring
Virginia artisans

JAMESTOWN GLASSHOUSE
Historic Jamestowne
1176 Jamestown Road
757-229-2437
Handblown glass items

PERIOD DESIGN
401 Main Street
Yorktown
757-886-9482
Seventeenth-century to
contemporary art and antiques

PRINCE GEORGE ART & FRAME
Colony Square Shopping Center
1303 Jamestown Road
757-229-7644
Fine art gallery and custom
framing

STUDIO FORAY
Riverwalk Landing
323 Water Street, Suite A4
Yorktown
757-969-1094
Unique custom-designed
jewelry

**THIS CENTURY ART
GALLERY**
219 N. Boundary Street
757-229-4949
Contemporary art and crafts

TK ARTS, INC.
1654 Jamestown Road
757-229-7988
Asian antiquities from the
seventeenth to nineteenth
centuries

A TOUCH OF EARTH
6580 Richmond Road
757-565-0425
American crafts and art

VICCELLIO GOLDSMITH
Riverwalk Landing
325 Water Street
Yorktown
757-890-2162
Fine jewelry

RECREATION

$\mathcal{T}$he Historic Triangle offers all sorts of outdoor and indoor activities, from award-winning golf courses to ghost tours. For those who like to walk or jog or bike, there are numerous trails and scenic routes in and around the Historic Area. (The Historic Area has a variety of surfaces, including cobblestones, shells, grass, and pavement, so wear supportive shoes.) And the area's rivers, once the lifeline for Indians and settlers, continue to be ideal for fishing and boating.

For more information on area parks, go to the following Web sites:

www.james-city.va.us/recreation

www.williamsburgva.gov/dept/rec/parks.htm

www.yorkcounty.gov/parksandrec/parks/parks_home.htm

www.dcr.state.va.us/parks/yorkrive.htm

GOLF

Back in 1724, Hugh Jones described a grueling expedition to the Virginia frontier, one that used up many a horseshoe. When the men returned, according to Jones, Gov. Alexander Spotswood presented each with a golden horseshoe. Like Spotswood's explorers, golfers who play the award-winning courses of Colonial Williamsburg's **Golden Horseshoe Golf Club**—listed as one of *Golf Magazine*'s "Top 100 You Can Play"—face a challenging test in a beautiful setting, one designated as an Audubon sanctuary. Renowned golf course architect Robert Trent Jones Sr. called the Gold Course his "finest" design, and *Golf Magazine* agreed, bestowing upon the course its prestigious Gold Medal award. The Green Course, designed by Rees Jones (Jones Sr.'s son), is carved from the same terrain but is longer and more forgiving. The Spotswood Course is the elder Jones's 1963 update of the Williamsburg Inn's original 1947 nine-hole course. To book your tee time, call (757) 220-7696.

WILLIAMSBURG AREA GOLF COURSES

FORD'S COLONY COUNTRY CLUB
240 Ford's Colony Drive
three courses consistently ranked among Virginia's best
757-258-4100

GOLDEN HORSESHOE GOLF CLUB
401 S. England Street
"one of the 50 best in the nation" *Condé Nast Traveler*
757-220-7696

KINGSMILL RESORT
1010 Kingsmill Road
River Course, home to the LPGA Tour's Michelob Ultra Open;
    Plantation Course designed by Arnold Palmer; Woods Course
    designed by Tom Clark
757-253-3906

TRADITION GOLF CLUB AT KISKIACK
8104 Club Drive
one of the area's newest championship courses
757-566-2200
800-989-4728

TRADITION GOLF CLUB AT STONEHOUSE
9700 Mill Pond Run
mountain-style course, four and a half stars from *Golf Digest*
757-566-1138
888-825-3436

WILLIAMSBURG NATIONAL GOLF CLUB
3700 Centerville Road
Nicklaus design, four and a half stars from *Golf Digest*
757-258-9642
800-826-5732

THE SPA OF COLONIAL WILLIAMSBURG: A CONTINUUM OF WELLNESS

A 20,000-square-foot luxury spa is located between the Williamsburg Inn and the Williamsburg Lodge and is just a chip shot from the Golden Horseshoe Golf Club.

The comprehensive spa, fitness center, and indoor pool complex contains twelve treatment areas and features the latest equipment. The facility also includes a hair and nail salon, dressing rooms, and lounge and dining areas. Wood, stone, and local materials create warm, natural interiors.

From practices based on Native American rituals to the botanicals of the colonial era to the revolutionary antiaging advancements of the twenty-first century, the therapies have withstood the test of time or the rigorous testing of today's clinical laboratories.

The Spa of Colonial Williamsburg presents each therapy in a relaxing, luxurious setting, pampering and nurturing guests. The experience invites each person to move along his or her own continuum of wellness.

For more information, call 1-800-688-6479.

EVENING ENTERTAINMENT

The Historic Area remains full of activity even after the sun goes down. Colonial Williamsburg's many programs include ghost tours; courtroom dramas featuring accused pirates and witches; concerts of period music; colonial dancing; and the "Grand Medley of Entertainments," a re-creation of an eighteenth-century traveling show that combines circus, carnival, and vaudeville elements. For the latest listings, check "This Week," a free Colonial Williamsburg publication. Many performances require separate tickets that can be purchased at any Colonial Williamsburg ticket sales location.

In addition to the "Grand Medley of Entertainments," the Kimball Theatre, at Merchants Square, presents performing arts, events, educational presentations, and films. For information, call (757)

565-8588 or 1-800-HISTORY or visit www.colonialwilliamsburg.com.

Outside the Historic Area, there's also plenty to amuse you, including bowling, pool, dinner theater, miniature golf, theater, and movies. For more information, go to www.visitwilliamsburg.com.

TRAVEL TIPS

GETTING TO THE TRIANGLE

AIRPORTS

NEWPORT NEWS/WILLIAMSBURG INTERNATIONAL AIRPORT

About thirty minutes from Williamsburg; served by AirTran, Delta, and US Airways

www.flynewportnews.com

757-877-0221

NORFOLK INTERNATIONAL AIRPORT

About an hour's drive from Williamsburg; served by American Airlines, Continental Airlines, Delta, Northwest Airlines, Southwest Airlines, United Express, and US Airways

www.norfolkairport.com

757-857-3351

RICHMOND INTERNATIONAL AIRPORT

About fifty minutes from Williamsburg; served by AirTran, American Airlines, Continental Airlines, Delta, Jet Blue Airways, Northwest Airlines, United, and US Airways

www.flyrichmond.com

804-226-3000

WILLIAMSBURG-JAMESTOWN AIRPORT

Private planes, air charters, air tours

www.wjairport.com

757-229-9256

WILLIAMSBURG TRANSPORTATION CENTER

Located four blocks from Colonial Williamsburg's Historic Area, the center serves as a train and bus station. Taxi and car rental companies also operate out of the center.

468 N. Boundary Street

www.ci.williamsburg.va.us/gen/direct/train.htm

AMTRAK

www.amtrak.com

800-872-7245

757-229-8750

GREYHOUND

www.greyhound.com

800-231-2222

757-229-1460

GETTING TO THE SITES

The Colonial Parkway connects all three points of the Historic Triangle. From within the Triangle, the parkway is generally the best way to reach Jamestown, Williamsburg, or Yorktown, and its scenic views make it a destination in its own right. Directions to the main sites from Interstate 64 are provided below.

HISTORIC JAMESTOWNE

From Richmond, take exit 238. Follow Route 143 east for a half mile. Turn right onto Route 132. Go about a mile and a half. Turn left onto Route 132Y (Visitor Center Drive). Continue past the Colonial Williamsburg Visitor Center on your left to the Colonial Parkway just ahead. Take a right at the stop sign onto the parkway. Follow the parkway to the entrance to Historic Jamestowne (about nine miles).

From Hampton Roads/Norfolk, take exit 242A to Route 199 west. Go three and a half miles to the second traffic light. Turn right onto South Henry Street. Make an immediate right onto the ramp onto the Colonial Parkway. Follow the parkway to the entrance to Historic Jamestowne (about seven miles).

JAMESTOWN SETTLEMENT

From Richmond, take exit 238. Follow Route 143 east for a half mile. Turn right onto Route 132. Go about a mile and a half. Turn left onto Route 132Y (Visitor Center Drive). Continue past the Colonial Williamsburg Visitor Center on your left to the Colonial Parkway just ahead. Take a right at the stop sign onto the parkway. Follow the parkway about nine miles. When you see the entrance to Historic Jamestowne, turn right onto Route 359. Jamestown Settlement will be on your left.

From Hampton Roads/Norfolk, take exit 242A to Route 199 west. Go three and a half miles to the second traffic light. Turn right onto South Henry Street. Make an immediate right onto the ramp onto the Colonial Parkway. Follow the parkway about seven miles. When you see the entrance to Historic Jamestowne, turn right onto Route 359. Jamestown Settlement will be on your left.

COLONIAL WILLIAMSBURG

Take exit 238. Follow Route 143 east for a half mile. Turn right onto Route 132. Go about a mile and a half. Turn left onto Route 132Y (Vistor Center Drive). The Colonial Williamsburg Visitor Center will be on your left.

Yorktown Battlefield

From Richmond, take exit 238. Follow Route 143 east for a half mile. Turn right onto Route 132. Go about a mile and a half. Turn left onto Route 132Y (Visitor Center Drive). Continue past the Colonial Williamsburg Visitor Center on your left to the Colonial Parkway just ahead. Take a left at the stop sign onto the parkway. Follow the parkway to its end (about thirteen miles) where signs will direct you to the battlefield.

From Hampton Roads/Norfolk, take exit 250B. At the end of the off-ramp, take a left at the traffic light onto Route 143 (Jefferson Avenue). Take your first right onto Route 105 (Fort Eustis Boulevard). In about three and a half miles, turn left onto Route 17. Take Route 17 approximately three miles. Turn left onto the entrance ramp for the Colonial Parkway. Turn left onto the parkway and follow it less than a mile to its end where signs will direct you to the battlefield.

Yorktown Victory Center

From Richmond, take exit 238. Follow Route 143 east for a half mile. Turn right onto Route 132. Go about a mile and a half. Turn left onto Route 132Y (Visitor Center Drive). Continue past the Colonial Williamsburg Visitor Center on your left to the Colonial Parkway just ahead. Take a left at the stop sign onto the parkway. Follow the parkway to the sign for the Victory Center (about twelve miles). Turn left. The Victory Center will be at the end of the off-ramp.

From Hampton Roads/Norfolk, take exit 250B. At the end of the off-ramp, take a left at the traffic light onto Route 143 (Jefferson Avenue). Take your first right onto Route 105 (Fort Eustis Boulevard). In about three and a half miles, turn left onto Route 17. Take Route 17 approximately three miles. Turn left onto the entrance ramp for the Colonial Parkway. Turn right onto the parkway. Follow the parkway less than a mile. At the sign for the Victory Center, turn right. The Victory Center is at the end of the off-ramp.

SHUTTLES AND BUSES
YORKTOWN TROLLEY

At Yorktown, the free **Yorktown Trolley** provides continuous service seasonally between the Yorktown Battlefield Visitor Center and the Yorktown Victory Center with stops at town sites.

WILLIAMSBURG AREA TRANSIT

Bus service to Colonial Williamsburg, Busch Gardens, the Pottery, Prime Outlets, and the College of William and Mary

www.williamsburgtransport.com

757-259-4093

WILLIAMSBURG TAXIS

HISTORIC TAXI

757-258-7755

YELLOW CAB OF WILLIAMSBURG

757-722-1111

WILLIAMSBURG CAR RENTALS

COLONIAL AND B&W RENT-A-CAR

468 N. Boundary Street

www.colonialrentacar.com

757-220-3399

800-899-2271

ENTERPRISE RENT-A-CAR

www.enterprise.com

6532 Richmond Road

757-258-9199

713 Merrimac Trail

757-220-1900

Operating Hours

Historic Jamestowne

Entrance open daily 8:30 a.m. to 4:30 p.m.; Visitor Center open daily 9 a.m. to 5 p.m.; Glasshouse open daily 8:30 a.m. to 5 p.m.; grounds, including archaeological site and tour roads, open daily until dusk. Closed Thanksgiving, Christmas, and New Year's Days.

Jamestown Settlement

Open daily 9 a.m. to 5 p.m. (6 p.m. June 15 through August 15). Closed Christmas and New Year's Days.

Colonial Williamsburg

Open 365 days a year. Most Historic Area sites are open 9 a.m. to 5 p.m. with special programming in the evening. For specific sites or programs, consult Colonial Williamsburg's "This Week" or call 1-800-HISTORY.

Yorktown Battlefield

Visitor Center open daily 9 a.m. to 5 p.m.; grounds open daily until dusk. Closed Thanksgiving, Christmas, and New Year's Days.

Yorktown Victory Center

Open daily 9 a.m. to 5 p.m. (6 p.m. June 15 through August 15). Closed Christmas and New Year's Days.

Useful Web Sites

Historic Jamestowne: www.historicjamestowne.org or
www.nps.gov/colo

Jamestown Settlement: www.historyisfun.org

Colonial Williamsburg: www.history.org

Yorktown Battlefield: www.nps.gov/colo

Yorktown Victory Center: www.historyisfun.org

America's Historic Triangle: www.historictriangle.com

America's four hundredth anniversary:
www.jamestown2007.org

Local Newspapers

Williamsburg's *Virginia Gazette*, first published in 1736, comes out twice a week and includes listings of local events. The *Daily Press*, based in Newport News, also covers the Historic Triangle.

Weather and Clothing

Winters are generally mild but occasionally very cold with average highs in the low 50s and average lows in the low 30s.

Spring and fall days are generally very pleasant although it can get hot or cold. Average highs climb from 61 in March to 71 in April, 78 in May, and 83 in June. Average lows rise from 37 in March to 44 in April, 54 in May, and 62 in June. Average highs fall from 82 in September to 71 in October and 62 in November. Average lows fall from 60 in September to 48 in October to 39 in November.

Summers are often hot and humid with average highs reaching 89 in July and 87 in August.

Average precipitation ranges from a little more than three inches a month in April, June, November, and December to more than five inches in July and just under five inches in August and September.

In general, dress is casual, though the Williamsburg Inn's Regency Room requires a tie and jacket for dinner. Almost all sites require some walking, and some on uneven pavements, so wear comfortable shoes.

WILLIAMSBURG MEDICAL SERVICES
Hospital
SENTARA WILLIAMSBURG REGIONAL MEDICAL CENTER
100 Sentara Circle
Lightfoot
757-984-6000

WALK-IN CARE
MEDEXPRESS
120 Monticello Avenue
757-564-3627
NEW TOWN URGENT CARE
4374 New Town Avenue
757-259-1900
RIVERSIDE WILLIAMSBURG MEDICAL ARTS–URGENT CARE
5231 John Tyler Highway
757-220-8300
FIRST MED OF WILLIAMSBURG
312 2nd Street
757-229-4141

ACCESSIBILITY
JAMESTOWN SETTLEMENT AND YORKTOWN VICTORY CENTER
All areas of the museums, except on board the ships at Jamestown Settlement, are wheelchair accessible. Restrooms are also wheelchair accessible. Strollers and wheelchairs are available on a first-come, first-served basis.

Open-captioned versions of on-site films are shown, and assistive listening systems are available on request. Sign language interpreters are available with a minimum two weeks' advance notice. Licensed guide animals assisting guests are allowed throughout the museums.

For more information:
(757) 253-4838
1-888-593-4682

COLONIAL WILLIAMSBURG

Colonial Williamsburg's Visitor Center, hotels, restaurants, and shops are largely accessible, and staff members will make special accommodations when necessary. Special parking arrangements are available for easier access to the Historic Area.

A limited number of folding wheelchairs, rented on a first-come first-served basis, are available at the Visitor Center. No motorized chairs are available.

The nature of the Historic Area and its eighteenth-century architecture may impose certain restrictions on some guests. On the other hand, the Historic Area offers the advantage of very few curbs, and automobiles are not permitted on the main street during the day. Costumed interpreters in the Historic Area will be glad to provide directions to accessible areas.

Most of the restored and reconstructed buildings in the Historic Area have entrance steps, but most interior doorways are wide enough to accommodate a wheelchair. Many of the exhibition buildings have second floors that are interpreted, and stairs are often steep and narrow. Where a program is not accessible, alternate interpretation may be available upon request.

Wheelchair-accessible restrooms are located in the Visitor Center, in the Merchants Square information station, at Bassett Hall, in the Public Hospital and the Colonial Williamsburg Art Museums, and in the Historic Area near the Guardhouse on Francis Street, on Botetourt Street between Duke of Gloucester and Nicholson Streets, and on the Palace grounds.

Licensed guide dogs are permitted in all Colonial Williamsburg buildings. Guests with visual impairments may make use of a headset sound track that describes the on-screen action in the movie *The Story of a Patriot*. Ask the usher for assistance in setting up the headset. Guests with visual impairments may also make advance arrangements for an escort by writing the visitor services coordinator (see below).

The publication "Colonial Williamsburg: A Guide for Deaf and

Hearing Impaired Visitors" is available free of charge at the Visitor Center. A printed synopsis of *The Story of a Patriot* is available at the Visitor Center, as are headsets with adjustable volume control. The east theater has a rear screen projection system that allows guests seated in any one of thirty seats to see a captioned version of the film by way of a mirror. Headsets with adjustable volume control are also available for lecture programs in the Hennage Auditorium at the De-Witt Wallace Decorative Arts Museum and at the Kimball Theatre. With two weeks' advance notice, Colonial Williamsburg can arrange for signing interpreters to accompany guests with hearing impairments through the Historic Area; please write the visitor services coordinator (see below). Hearing dogs are permitted in all buildings.

For more specific information on the accessibility of particular sites in the Historic Area, please visit www.history.org/accessibility/list.cfm or contact the visitor services coordinator:

Visitor Services Coordinator
Visitor Center Administrative Office
Colonial Williamsburg Foundation
101A Visitor Center Drive
Williamsburg, Virginia 23185
(757) 220-7645
1-800-246-2099

Historic Jamestowne and Yorktown Battlefield

Wheelchairs are available on a first-come, first-served basis. Restrooms are wheelchair accessible. Some paths are not wheelchair accessible. Citizens and permanent residents of the United States who have disabilities are entitled to an America the Beautiful Access Pass, which provides free admission to National Park Service sites. Documentation of blindness or permanent disability is required.

For more information:
(757) 898-2410

Image Credits

Anheuser-Busch, 9, 202, 203, 204 top and bottom. Berkeley Plantation, 206. Charlottesville/Albemarle Convention and Visitors Bureau, 227. Chrysler Museum, 214 top. The Colonial Williamsburg Foundation, 14–15, 22, 50, 51 top, 51 bottom (bequest of Mrs. Edward S. Harkness), 53 (gift of Joseph R. Lasser), 59 (acquisition funded by John D. Rockefeller Jr.), 60 (gift of John D. Rockefeller Jr.), 64, 65 (gift of the Vestry of Bruton Parish Church), 68–69, 76–77, 78–79, 100–101, 114–115, 122–123 (gift of Abby Aldrich Rockefeller), 130, 131, 132, 133, 134, 135. Jamestown-Yorktown Foundation, 16 top, 26–27, 28–29, 30, 31 top, 32, 32–33, 34, 35, 82–83, 109, 112 top and bottom, 113, 116 top and bottom, 117 all, 118, 119, 121, 124, 125, 126, 127, 197 top and bottom, 198, 200. Library of Congress, 55 top and bottom. Eric Lindberg/Richmond Metropolitan Convention and Visitors Bureau, 222 top. Mariners' Museum, 66–67, 192–193, 209. Monticello/Thomas Jefferson Foundation, Inc., 226. National Archives, 80. National Park Service, 42–43 (cannon), 104 top, 106 bottom, 181, 186, 187, 188 top, 190. National Portrait Gallery, Smithsonian Institution, 61. Norfolk Department of Development, 214 bottom, 215. Jodi Norman, 47. Preservation Virginia, 13 (1590 copper token), 18–19, 19, 21 top (axe, adze, and croze from Jamestown), 25, 26, 27, 31 bottom, 37, 86 bottom three, 94, 95 top and bottom, 96 bottom, 97, 98, 99, 104 bottom, 219, 221, 229, 230. Richmond Metropolitan Convention and Visitors Bureau, 220 top, 222 bottom, 223, 224. Right Minds/Richmond Metropolitan Convention and Visitors Bureau, 220 bottom. Shirley Plantation in Charles City, Virginia, 207. United States Army, 211. Virginia Air and Space Center, 212, 213. Virginia Beach Convention and Visitors Bureau, 217, 218. Virginia Historical Society, 56. Additional photos by Colonial Williamsburg staff photographers David M. Doody, Tom Green, Barbara Lombardi, Lael White, and Kelly J. Mihalcoe.

Acknowledgments

For their invaluable assistance, thanks to Jamestown 2007, the Jamestown-Yorktown Foundation, the National Park Service, Preservation Virginia, and the following divisions and departments at the Colonial Williamsburg Foundation: Archaeological Research, Architectural Research, Archives, Commercial Properties, Historic Trades, Hospitality, Internet, Marketing, Museums, Photo Services, Print Production Services, Products, Public History, Research, and the John D. Rockefeller, Jr. Library. Thanks also to Blair A. Rudes and special thanks to Lloyd Dobyns. "Practical Information" listings courtesy of the Williamsburg Area Restaurant Association and the Greater Williamsburg Chamber & Tourism Alliance.

INDEX